FULL GOSPEL CHURCH LIBRARY
KELOWNA, B.C.

WHEN THE CHURCH WAS
YOUNG

*L*UMINAIRE *S*TUDIES

WHEN THE CHURCH WAS YOUNG

Studies in the Thessalonian Epistles

DAVID EWERT

Kindred Press

Winnipeg, MB Canada   Hillsboro, KS U.S.A.

When the Church Was Young
Copyright © 1993 by David Ewert, Abbotsford, BC.

All rights reserved. With the exception of brief excerpts for reviews, no part of this book may be reproduced without written permission of the publisher.

Scripture taken from the **HOLY BIBLE: NEW INTERNATIONAL VERSION** R. **NIV** R. Copyright © 1973, 1978, 1984 by International Bible Society. Used by permission of Zondervan Publishing House.

Published simultaneously by Kindred Press, Winnipeg. Manitoba R2L 2E5 and Kindred Press, Hillsboro, Kansas 67063

Cover design by Lee Toews, TS Design Associates, Winnipeg
Book design by Publishing Services, Winnipeg
Printed in Canada by Derksen Printers, Steinbach, MB

Canadian Cataloguing in Publication Data
　　Ewert, David, 1922-

　　　　When the church was young
　　　　(Luminaire series)
　　　　Includes the text of the epistles.
　　　　ISBN: 0-921788-18-5

1. Bible. N.T. Thessalonians - Commentaries
I. Bible. N.T. Thessalonians. English. II. Title.
III. Series

BS2725.3.E93 1993　　227'.81077　　C93-098099-9

International Standard Book Number: 0-921788-18-5

PREFACE

Several years ago I wrote a commentary on the Thessalonian epistles for the *Evangelical Commentary on the Bible*, published by Baker Book House. That volume runs to over 1200 pages and is not likely to become household reading. The present book is designed specifically for Bible study groups and classes and resembles other commentaries in the *Luminaire* series. Commentaries are no substitutes for the Bible, but they are designed to help us understand the Bible better.

The text of the two Thessalonian epistles has been divided into thirteen chapters and can be covered in one quarter of the church year. At the end of each chapter the reader will find review questions which should help in the discussion of the passages under study.

The biblical text, quoted in full at the beginning of each chapter, is from the New International Version. The outlines in this commentary may not be the kind a preacher would use in a sermon, but they reflect the subject matter in the epistles and should contribute to an orderly study of the biblical text.

Like other volumes in the *Luminaire* series this commentary is non-technical. Scholars throughout the twentieth century have produced a great many expositions of the Thessalonian letters, in various languages. English commentaries range from the rather more technical, such as George Milligan's, to the more popular, such as William Barclay's. They all have their place, but often have a different set of readers in mind.

Although I have tried to pay careful attention to the Greek text of these ancient letters of Paul, I have left aside numerous critical questions and concentrated on the meaning of Paul's message to the church in the first century and on its relevance today.

It may well be that the Thessalonian letters are the earliest documents we have from the pen of the apostle Paul (unless Galatians should be earlier). In our Bibles, however, they stand at the end of the collection of Paul's letters to the churches. That's because they are ordered according to length in our canon, beginning with Romans and ending with 2nd Thessalonians.

Paul was a church planter and most of his letters are addressed to young churches which he had planted, by the grace of God. For that reason I have chosen the title: When the Church Was Young. Since these documents are part of the living and abiding word of God, they continue to inform, correct and encourage us in our daily life and mission, even though they were written nearly two thousand years ago.

David Ewert

TABLE OF CONTENTS

I Thessalonians

1. A Joyful Greeting (1 Thess. 1:1-3) 1
2. A New Life in Christ (1 Thess. 1:4-10) 11
3. In the Service of Christ (1 Thess. 2:1-12) 21
4. Church Planting, First Century Style (1 Thess. 2:13-3:13) 33
5. Pleasing God in Everyday Life (1 Thess. 4:1-12) . . . 47
6. The Blessed Hope of the Church (1 Thess. 4:13-18) . . 59
7. Christ's Coming at the End of the Age (1 Thess.5:1-11) 69
8. The Spiritual Life of the Church (1 Thess. 5:12-28) . . 79

II Thessalonians

1. The Judgment at Christ's Coming (2 Thess. 1:3-12) . . 93
2. The Coming of the Lawless One (2 Thess. 2:1-i2) . . 109
3. Exhortation to Steadfastness (2 Thess. 2:13-17) . . . 123
4. A Prayer for Mission (2 Thess. 3:1-5) 131
5. An Orderly Christian Life (2 Thess. 3:6-15) 139
Bibliography 151

CHAPTER ONE

A JOYFUL GREETING

> *Paul, Silas and Timothy, to the church of the Thessalonians, who are in God the Father and the Lord Jesus Christ: Grace and peace to you. We always thank God for all of you, mentioning you in our prayers. We continually remember before our God and Father your work produced by faith, your labor prompted by love, and your endurance inspired by hope in our Lord Jesus Christ (1 Thess. 1:1-3).*

The city of Thessalonica lay on a major Roman highway which ran through Macedonia to the west coast. Paul and his colleagues came here from Philippi where, in spite of much suffering, they were able to establish a church. There was evidently a sizeable Jewish population in Thessalonica and, as was his custom, Paul proclaimed Christ in the Jewish synagogue on several sabbaths until he was forced out.

The missionaries supported themselves so that the Thessalonians would not be burdened by them, and witnessed to the saving grace of God. Because a goodly number of people who frequented the synagogue became Christians, the Jewish leaders made life difficult for the missionaries. Under the influence of leading Jews, the rabble assaulted the house of Jason with whom Paul was staying. And when they failed to find Paul at his house they dragged Jason before the magistrates. Jason was forced to pay security and to promise not to cause further trouble. Since it was no longer feasible to continue with their teaching and preaching ministry in

Thessalonica Paul and his companions left for Beroea, leaving the young Thessalonian church without apostolic guidance.

After establishing another church in Beroea, Jews from Thessalonica came to Beroea and harassed Paul and his associates. As a result, Paul and Timothy (where Silas stayed is not clear) moved on to Athens. From here Paul sent his faithful colleague, Timothy, back to Thessalonica to see how the church was faring. Meantime he settled in Corinth, and there the good news reached him through Timothy that the church was standing firm in its new faith in spite of persecution. Although evil rumors were being spread about the apostles by the enemies of the gospel, the Thessalonians remembered the missionaries kindly. However, there were still many gaps in the knowledge of this young church about the Christian life. And so Paul writes to the Thessalonians, thanking God for the miracle of grace that had taken place in their lives, and instructing them further in the things of God. We begin our study of this letter by examing Paul's joyful greeting.

I. The Apostolic Source of the Greeting (1:1a).

A. The Writer.

Paul, the apostle, is the writer of this letter. All of his letters begin more or less like other letters in his day, with the name of the author, the identity of the person addressed, and the greeting. Following the standard letter-writing form does not mean, however, that there are no unique features in Paul's greetings. Whereas the Gospel writers created a new literary genre, the apostles had well-established models of epistolary forms which they could follow.

First Thessalonians begins with a short prescript. In most of his letters Paul adds an appositive to his name, such as "apostle", but here we have only his name. He uses the name *Paulos*, by which he was known in the Greco-Roman world. Were it not for the book of Acts we would not even know that he also had a name by which he was known in Jewish circles, namely Saul. It was not uncommon in Paul's day for Jews to have two names—one by which they were known in the Jewish community, another in society at large.

B. His Associates.

Paul associates Silas (the Greek text uses the Latin form "Silvanus") and Timothy with himself in his preface. They had been part of the missionary team that planted the gospel in Thessalonica and so it was only natural that he should mention them in his letters to the Thessalonians. It does not follow, however, that they participated in the writing of these epistles. Silas and Timothy are mentioned as a courteous gesture, since they were well-known to the readers. Although the plural "we" occurs several times in this letter, Paul also uses the singular "I" (2:18; 3:5; 5:27), and so we must assume that he alone is the writer, even though he may have shared the contents of this letter with his associates.

Silas was a member of the Jerusalem church. Together with three other men he conveyed the apostolic decree to the Antiochian church (Acts 15:22ff.). He then accompanied Paul on his so-called second missionary journey in the place of Barnabas, who was with Paul on his first journey. The practice of sending teams of two or three probably had its background in the Old Testament emphasis on establishing the truth on the basis of two or three witnesses. Jesus also sent out his disciples two by two.

Timothy was a younger associate. He was one of Paul's converts and joined the missionary party at Lystra (Acts 16:1-3). Although his name does not occur in Luke's account of the founding of the Thessalonian church, we must assume that he was with Paul and Silas at the time, as was Luke himself. He was a faithful emissary of Paul and in six of his thirteen letters Paul mentions him alongside his own name. Timothy's name occurs in all of Paul's letters except

Galatians and Ephesians.

Paul had the good fortune of having trustworthy colleagues and repeatedly in his letters he pays tribute to them. Here, however, just as in his own case, Paul says nothing beyond their names. The number and quality of Paul's companions in the work of the kingdom are an index to his own character. Although Paul strikes us as a pioneer, he leaned heavily upon his friends, and he paid them high compliments.

II. The Christian Recipients of the Greeting (1 -1b).

The letter is addressed to "the church of the Thessalonians." When we use the word "church" we immediately think of a Christian community, but in Paul's day the word *ekklesia* was used for any summoned assembly, religious or secular. The Septuagint uses this Greek word to designate the assembly of the people of God in the Old Testament. The word, then, as used by Paul, has a double background: in everyday life it was the word used for any kind of summoned gathering of people; but it also has a religious background in the history of the Jewish people.

The meaning of the word *ekklesia* is not that different from synagogue, but Christian believers preferred to use *ekklesia* for their gatherings, and so synagogue was restricted more and more to Jewish assemblies. *Ekklesia* is used to designate a local body of believers (as in our text), but it can also designate the entire body of Christ, the universal church. The word does not in its earlier stages refer to a building, as the word "church" does in English. The emphasis in New Testament times is entirely on the people who comprise the Christian community, rather than a building in which they meet.

That Paul is addressing a Christian assembly in Thessalonica is underscored by the addition, "in God the Father and the Lord Jesus Christ." God and Christ are linked in such a way as to suggest that for Paul, Jesus is divine.

Twenty years after the resurrection of Jesus, Christians without embarrassment put him on the same level with God.

To be "in" God the Father and "in" the Lord Jesus Christ would suggest that the church has its source and origin in divine activity, and that its existence here on earth is determined by God, and that the members live in fellowship with God the Father and the Lord Jesus Christ.

III. The Standard Form of Greeting (1:1c).

"Grace to you and peace," concludes the prescript of this letter. It is the standard Pauline greeting, although it is somewhat abbreviated in our text. In his second letter to the Thessalonias Paul adds "from God our Father and the Lord Jesus Christ," and so it happens that some Greek manuscripts and ancient versions have that addition also in I Thessalonians. People who spoke Greek might greet each other with the word *chairein* ("rejoice," "hail"), and this is the word used in two letters in Acts (15:23;23:26) and in the letter of James (1:1). By a slight linguistic shift Paul changes the word to *charis* (grace). It is a key-word in Pauline theology and speaks of that unmerited favor and kindness which God has demonstrated in sending his Son to give life and hope to all who believe in him.

"Peace" is the standard Jewish greeting. Behind the Greek word for peace (*eirene*) stands the Old Testament word "shalom," which means much more than the absence of strife; it includes well-being, fullness of life, and salvation. In one sense these two words give us the gist of the gospel. One might think of them as the greetings of the Gentile and Jewish world, informed and deepened by the fact that God in Christ has redeemed the world and now offers his grace and salvation to all humankind. If the order of the two words is significant, then one might say that the peace of God flows into people's lives when they experience God's redeeming grace. These two words would evoke thoughts of God's undeserving favor in the minds of the readers, and move them to gratitude for the spiritual wholeness that had come to them through the message of the gospel.

IV. The Genuine Sincerity of the Greeting (1:2).

"We always thank God for all of you." We can only imagine what an impression such words from the pen of the apostle must have had on the readers. Although letters in Paul's day regularly began with a thanksgiving, the apostle's thanks to God for the Thessalonians is not a mere formality. It comes from a heart of love for his converts.

The plural "we" may be simply literary, however, if taken in a more literal sense it could mean that Paul and his colleagues regularly thanked God for the Thessalonians. The word "always" must not of course be understood to mean that Paul and his associates never did anything else. It may in fact be connected with "making mention" in the sense that whenever Paul prays for them he also thanks God for his converts in Thessalonica.

He thanks God not simply for the leaders of the church, or for some prominent members, but for "all" of them. How many of them he knew by name is hard to say, but he excludes no one from his expression of thanks. There were those in Thessalonica who fell short of the standards of the Christian life as taught by the apostles, but Paul has a sharp eye for what God's grace has accomplished in every believer.

That the readers had weaknesses and needs is obvious from the fact that the apostles continually make mention of them in their prayers. Whether they mentioned their converts by name when they prayed, or whether they made mention of their needs, their temptations, their difficulties, is not clear. However, one of the tests of a person's genuine concern for others is intercessary prayer. And one doesn't need to know all the answers to the questions about intercession to continue to intercede for our fellow believers.

V. The Specific Reasons for the Greeting (1:3)

"We continually remember before our God and Father your work produced by faith, your labor prompted by love, and your endurance inspired by hope in our Lord Jesus Christ." Memory plays an important role in the Christian life. Ungrateful believers suffer from short memories. "Forget not all his benefits," is the exhortation of the Psalmist. As we remember people we are prompted to thank God and to pray for them.

What was it that the apostles remembered specifically as they reflected on their ministry in Thessalonica? They remembered expressions of the three most eminent Christian graces: faith, love and hope. This triad is found repeatedly in Paul (cf. Rom. 5:1-5; Gal. 5:5f.; 1 Thess. 5:8; etc.) but also in non-Pauline writings (Heb. 6:10-12; 10:22-24; 1 Pet. 1:3-8). These three graces are a kind of compendium of the Christian life in the eyes of the apostles. Faith, love and hope express the essence of the new life in Christ.

Faith, love and hope, however, are not abstract qualities of the Christian life; they express themselves concretely. Faith shows itself in work, love in labor, hope in waiting for Christ to return. In one sense it could be said that faith looks to the past—to the finished work of Christ, love to the present—expressing itself in useful labor for others, and hope looks to the future, to the last day when history will be wrapped up and we shall enter the eternal kingdom. Let us look at these aspects of the Christian life a bit more specifically!

A. The Work of Faith.

In some of his letters (e.g. Galatians) Paul seems to put faith and works into antithesis. And when "works" represent human efforts at attaining salvation they must be condemned as inadequate. Martin Luther put faith and works into such a radical disjunction that he could hardly appreciate the emphasis on works as found in the Epistle of James. However, even in Galatians, in which works are condemned, Paul stresses the importance of "faith working through love" (5:6). And to the Ephesians he writes that we were created in Christ Jesus "for good works" (2:10).

"Work" in our passage is a comprehensive term for the practical dimensions of the Christian life which come from a living faith. It is by "work" that a genuine faith is authenticated. What all Paul had in mind when he used the word "work" to describe the activities of the Thessalonians is hard to say, but it would certainly embrace many of those activities by which believers help to build the kingdom of God

The word "faith" is used in more than one sense in the New Testament, but it is certainly not to be understood as the opposite of "thought." If there is an opposite to faith one could mention "sight," for we walk by faith and not by sight in this life. But to be a believer does not demand that we sacrifice our intellects. In fact, faith embraces our entire personality—our will, our emotions, our mind.

Sometimes "faith" is used in the sense of doctrine. "Earnestly contending for the faith" (Jude 3) lays the emphasis on true Christian teaching. When faith is listed with other fruits of the Spirit (Gal. 5:22), the meaning is probably that of faithfulness. Paul can even preach the faith (Gal. 1:23). Faith in that case stands by metonymy for the gospel. Basically, however, faith means trust, commitment, loyalty to Jesus. Faith is our response to the grace of God offered to us in the gospel, by which we receive deliverance from sin and guilt and the hope of eternal life. When a person puts his or her full trust in Christ for salvation, this faith expresses itself in holiness of life, in caring about others, in witness, in integrity, in loyalty to Jesus.

B. The Labor of Love.

The word "labor"(*kopos*) is stronger than the word "work"(*ergon*). It emphasizes exertion and the weariness that comes from sweaty toil. Etymologically the word comes from a verb (*kopto*) which means to strike or beat, and then "to be beat" as we say (to be tired). Paul frequently uses the word to describe his missionary labors (e.g. 1 Cor. 15:10; Gal. 4:11; Phil. 2:16). In 1 Thess. 2:9 it stands together with another word that stresses the weariness that stems from hard work.

Without such labors the work of the church would not be done. It is often unseen, unpaid and unrecognized. It springs from love (*agape*). Now it is tragically possible to be engaged in exhausting labor and yet have lost one's love (Rev. 2:4). One can labor out of a grim sense of duty, out of hope for material gain or human recognition but the Thessalonians, says Paul, labored out of love.

Agape is not simply a warm feeling in a person's heart, although it would be wrong to suggest that it is without warmth. But it has as much or more to do with a person's will as with his or her emotions. Having experienced the love of God in Christ in their own experience, the Thessalonians responded with a love that led them to spend themselves in the service of God.

C. The Endurance of Hope.

Endurance (*hupomone*) is one of the noblest words in the New Testament. It is not simply a human virtue, human fortitude in the face of difficulties and disasters, or natural toughness of character. On the other hand, it is not simply a kind of blithe optimism, either, that sees a silver lining in every cloud. "Endurance" in our text describes that patience, confidence and perseverance in a world that is hostile to the Christian faith.

Moreover, this endurance is inspired and sustained by the hope of the believer. It is not hope in general, but hope in the Lord Jesus Christ.

Hope in the New Testament is not simply wishful thinking; it is in fact very concrete. It is a hope that is laid up in heaven (Col. 1:5). We wait for this blessed hope (Tit. 2:13).

Christian hope is that confident expectation that God will wrap up human history in his own good time and bring his children into the eternal kingdom.

In his message to the church at Ephesus our Lord speaks so comfortingly: "I know your works (*erga*), your labor (*kopos*) and your endurance (*hupomone*)"(Rev. 2:2). His words serve as a succinct summary of what we have in our text. But how are we to understand "before our God and Father" in 1:3? To relate it to the word "remembering" is one possibility. Paul remembers these practical expressions of faith, love and hope in the life of the Thessalonians. But we could also relate the phrase to the word "hope," although that may be too restrictive. Perhaps their entire life in all its aspects could be seen as lived in the presence of God our Father.

Personal Response

1. *Paul pays tribute to many of his associates in his letters, both men and women. Do we make it easy or hard for others to work together with us in the kingdom of God?*
2. *What kind of range do we have in our intercessary prayers? Do we uphold individuals, churches, schools, mission and relief organizations in our prayers? And are our petitions laced with thanksgiving for people who are serving Christ?*
3. *Do we participate in the work of the church for personal gain or can we honestly say that it is our faith and our love that moves us to devote time, energy and money to the work of God's kingdom?*

CHAPTER TWO

THE NEW LIFE IN CHRIST

Brothers loved by God, we know that he has chosen you, because our gospel came to you not simply with words, but also with power, with the Holy Spirit and with deep conviction. You know how we lived among you for your sake. You became imitators of us and of the Lord; in spite of severe suffering, you welcomed the message with the joy given by the Holy Spirit. And so you became a model to all the believers in Macedonia and Achaia. The Lord's message rang out from you not only in Macedonia and Achaia—your faith in God has become known everywhere. Therefore we do not need to say anything about it, for they themselves report what kind of reception you gave us. They tell how you turned to God from idols to serve the living and true God, and to wait for his Son from heaven, whom he raised from the dead—Jesus who rescues us from the coming wrath (1 Thess. 4-10).

I. The Spiritual Roots of the New Life (1:4-6).

Paul and his associates are grateful for the work of grace that God had done in the lives of the Thessalonians. Their lives had been turned around, transformed by the gospel. Paul takes no credit for this miracle by which both Jews and Gentiles had become humble followers of Jesus. The secret of the new life in Christ is seen, ultimately, in the love of God which brought about the election of the Thessalonians.

A. Their Election by God.

"Brothers, beloved by God, we know that he has chosen you" (v. 4). The affectionate address, "brothers," suggests that Paul thought of the church as a family. Although the word was used both of Greek and Jewish "brotherhoods," Paul uses it as a designation for all believers (including women, for the word is used in its eclesial sense and not to differentiate genders). The word "brothers" is found no fewer than twenty-one times in these two Thessalonian Epistles alone.

The readers of this letter, so Paul affirms, were loved by God. The perfect participle of the verb (*egapemenoi*) suggests that God placed his love upon them and loves them still. And because of his love for them he chose them for himself. The word "election" (*ekloge*) is found only here in the New Testament, although there are several related words.

The concept of election has its background in the Old Testament where Israel is chosen of God to be his people by whom he wanted to bring salvation to the world. And just as Israel could not explain why God had chosen her from among the many nations, other than that he had loved Israel (Deut. 10:5), so it is with the saints of the New Testament, who have entered into Israel's heritage.

Election is a word that stresses that our salvation is entirely of God's grace. It leads us to worship, wonder and adore the God who chose us. It's a doctrine deeply appreciated by those who are in the family of God. "Elect," like "brothers," is a word of belonging, of community, of identity. Election speaks of the mystery of sovereign grace.

How did the apostles know that God had chosen the Thessalonians to be members of his family? No doubt by what was said in 1:3: "the work of faith, the labor of love, the endurance of hope." In Ephesians 1:4 Paul adds that the believers were chosen in Christ "before the foundation of the world." And having reached back into eternity, Paul now takes us into the moment of time when the gospel came to the Thessalonians and they heard of God's love and embraced the good news.

B. The Preaching of the Gospel by the Apostles.

"Because our gospel came to you not simply with words, but also with power, with the Holy Spirit and with deep conviction. You know how we lived among you for your sake"(v. 5). Paul speaks of "my gospel" (2 Tim. 2:8), "the gospel" (2 Thess. 1:8), "the gospel of God" (1 Thess. 2:9),"the gospel of Christ" (1 Thess. 3:2). Here he has "our gospel." The pronoun "our" must not be understood as if the apostles possessed the gospel or had an edge on it. But they had experienced the gospel themselves and had proclaimed it in Thessalonica.

"Gospel" (*euangelion*) means good news. Although it is used also in non-Christian contexts for good news in general, in the New Testament it designates the good news that God in Christ has brought about the salvation of the world. (The secular meaning of the verb *euangelizomai* can be found in 2 Thess. 3:6, where Timothy's report on the Thessalonians is called "good news.") The word *euangelion* is a favorite term of Paul for the Christian message and occurs some sixty times in his writings.

This gospel had come to the Thessalonians not only in word but also in power. Paul is not denying that the gospel was in fact proclaimed in word. In v. 8 he calls it "the word of the Lord." But it did not come in word only. Paul is not denigrating speech or the packaging of the Christian message in meaningful and attractive words. But eloquence alone does not change people's lives or make them followers of Jesus.

What is needed is, first of all, "power" (*dunamis*) and the Holy Spirit. The Spirit and power are almost a word-pair in Paul's letters. The Spirit takes lifeless human words and brings them home to the heart in such a powerful way that people open their hearts to hear the message of salvation.

Some think Paul has miracles in mind which characterized his ministry (Rom. 15:18), but then we might have expected the plural "powers." The apostle seems to have in mind here the internal operation of the Holy Spirit in power, convicting sinners of their need of a Savior, and opening their hearts to receive God's grace.

Also, the gospel came to the Thessalonians with "full conviction." This could be a reference to the fact that the missioners were fully convinced that the message they had to give was indeed the word of God. We will never be effective witnesses if we have doubts about the gospel. On the other hand, this may be a reference to the deep assurance that the Holy Spirit gave the Thessalonians that the message of the apostles was indeed trustworthy, a message on which they could stake their lives. This kind of assurance does not come by logical argument or scientific proof, but it is an inner conviction that the Holy Spirit brings to those who embrace the gospel by faith.

What gave credibility to the message proclaimed by the apostles was their everyday life. "You know how we lived among you for your sake." The gospel is communicated not only in word but also in life. One cannot be a good witness of the gospel and live in a manner that denies the gospel. If the gospel is to be believable our conduct must be consistant with what we proclaim.

In what may be the oldest sermon outside the New Testament (the *Shepherd of Hermas*) we read: "The Gentiles when they hear from our mouth the oracles of God, marvel at them for their beauty and greatness; then, when they discover that our works are not worthy of the words we speak, forthwith they betake themselves to blasphemy, saying that it is an idle story and delusion." That kind of charge the apostles were careful to prevent, and so they lived circumspectly.

C. The Response of the Readers.

"You became imitators of us and of the Lord; in spite

of severe suffering, you welcomed the message with the joy given by the Holy Spirit" (v. 6). Paul here becomes very personal. Election took place in eternity; the gospel came to them in the middle of the first century; but the new life in Christ began when they personally welcomed the good news.

To receive the word is another way of saying that they believed the gospel. "The word" is shorthand for the gospel. The Thessalonians received the word in spite of severe suffering. The gospel frequently arouses fierce hostility, especially in religious societies. There was considerable opposition to the apostles in Thessalonica, and their converts also had to suffer persecution. Nevertheless, they received the gospel with joy given by the Holy Spirit.

Tribulation and joy are often found going hand in hand in the experience of early Christians. From that it can be clearly seen that Christian joy is not simply the result of favorable circumstances. It is rather that deep inner assurance that our lives are in the hands of a loving Father who leads, even through suffering, to final glory. The source of the joy of Paul's readers was the Holy Spirit. In 1:5 we are told that the Holy Spirit gave power to the preachers and assurance to the believing hearers. Now we are told that he also gave them joy even in the midst of pain. "Joy" is a fruit of the Spirit (Gal. 5:22).

In their experience of persecution as well as in their holy joy they became imitators of the apostles. The word is *mimetai* (our "mimick") but should not be read as if the new converts began to imitate the apostles in the way they spoke, ate and dressed. However, the apostles modelled the Christian life for them. That was all the more significant at a time when the New Testament books had not yet been written, and the example of the missionaries and what they had taught them orally was all that the new Christians had to guide them.

And lest this should sound overbearing on the part of Paul to say that the Thessalonians imitated the messengers of the gospel, he quickly adds "and of the Lord." In 1 Corinthians 11:1 Paul is pleased that the Corinthians had imitated him just as he had imitated the Lord. What Paul had learned from Jesus he passed on to his converts.In 1:4-6 Paul has touched upon three springs of the new life in Christ: their election by God (v. 4); the preaching of the apostles (v. 5); and the response of the readers (v. 6). He will now recall how this new life manifested itself practically in Thessalonica.

II. The Practical Manifestations of the New Life (1:7-10).

A. Living Exemplary Lives.

"And so you became a model to all the believers in Macedonia and Achaia" (v. 7). After modelling their lives after the example of the apostles who, in turn, imitated our Lord, the Thessalonians themselves became models for other believers to follow. To speak of a church as an example, a model (*tupos* in Greek), is high praise.

The churches in Macedonia would include Philippi and Beroea we assume. In Achaia lay Athens, Corinth and Cenchraea (Rom. 16:1)—cities in which believers could be found. Macedonia and Achaia were the two Roman provinces of Greece at this time. Those who have done pioneer mission work know how important Christian examples are for young believers who are just learning to walk on the narrow road that leads to eternal life.

B. Spreading the Gospel.

"The Lord's message rang out from you not only in Macedonia and Achaia—your faith in God has become known everywhere. Therefore we do not need to say anything about it" (v. 8).

The word of the Lord, that is the gospel, "sounded forth" from these young converts. The verb *exechetai* (from which we derive the word "echo") suggests the sound of a trumpet or the sound of thunder, figuratively speaking. Having received the good news the Thessalonians were anxious to pass it on to others, and so their faith in God became known everywhere. "Everywhere" is obviously a hyperbolic expression, but it does suggest that the conversion of the Thessalonians was reported beyond the boundaries of Greece. People in Rome or in Ephesus may have heard the rumor of how God in his grace had created a new people of God in Thessalonica.

To say that their faith in God went out to every place is no different from saying that the word of the Lord "echoed" forth from them. The story of the conversion of the Thessalonians was spreading and when Paul came to a new place the rumor had preceded him and so he didn't need to tell about the miracle of God's grace in Thessalonica. This is still one of the most effective methods of evangelism: spreading the rumor of how God has changed the lives of people who embraced the gospel.

C. Serving the Living God.

"For they themselves report what kind of reception you gave us. They tell how you turned to God from idols to serve the living and true God" (v. 9).

What was it that people everywhere were hearing about the Thessalonians? According to v. 8 it was their faith in God. Secondly, it was the kind of reception they had given the missionaries. The word "reception" translates the Greek *eisodos*, which means quite literally "entrance." That could include the arrival and reception of the travelling witnesses, but it probably goes beyond the external circumstances of their visit to Thessalonica. It no doubt includes the response of the Thessalonians to the message of the gospel. Their visit in this city was not in vain, as Paul puts it in 2:1.

But the "holy gossip" about the Thessalonians that is making rounds in other cities includes another aspect: how they were converted from idols to serve the living God. The verb *epistrepho* ("turn") is one of the words for conversion in the Bible. It is very common in the book of Acts, but not with Paul. It's a metaphor that underscores the radical change in a person's life. It signifies a break with a sinful past. Specifically Paul mentions here the turning away from idols. That suggests that he has Gentiles in mind. It should not be overlooked, however, that he began his work in the Jewish synagogue and that there were Jewish converts in Thessalonica as well.

In contrast to dead idols Paul mentions the living God; and the true God stands over against false gods. Idols there are many, but there is only one true God. One might appropriately ask what people are converted from today, since idol worship in its literal sense is not generally practised in the Western world. But there are plenty of substitutes for God—money, power, and pride of position. Some people are possessed with politics, with sex, with sports or drugs. The human heart, wrote John Calvin, is an idol factory. The gods of ancient Greece and Rome tend to crop up in new dress again and again. And so we too, must be turned from idols if we want to serve the living and true God.

Conversion must not be thought of only in negative terms. To turn from idols is only one aspect of a living faith. The other is devotion to God. The word "to serve" in our text (*douleuo*) means literally to be a slave. Enslavement to idols is in one sense an involuntary slavery; we are captured by a power that gains control over us. But to be "enslaved" to God is a life of freedom, for this service is freely undertaken.

In the rumor that was spreading about the Thessalonians one other item was included: that they were now waiting for Jesus to return.

D. Waiting for the Son from Heaven.

"And to wait for his Son from heaven, whom he raised from the dead—Jesus, who rescues us from the coming wrath" (v. 10).

Serving the living God and waiting for his Son from heaven go hand in hand. Christians can get so caught up in waiting for the end of this age that they neglect their service in the world during this interim. Waiting doesn't mean that we sit and do nothing. If, for example, a housewife expects guests for dinner, she doesn't sit and wait for them. Rather she tidies up the house, peels the potatoes, sets the table, perhaps not even constantly thinking of the guests. But she's getting ready for the event. In the same way the believer seeks to fulfill his or her mission in this world, and that is the proper manner in which to wait for the Son from heaven. In keeping with its Hebrew background (in which "heaven" is always plural) Paul uses the plural here as well. The Hebrews thought of one heaven on top of another (Paul, on one occasion, was in the "third" heaven, 2 Cor. 12:2). Although "heaven" does at times mean the sky, here the reference is to the dwelling place of God.

It may be that the simple designation of Jesus as "Son" in our text is an abbreviation of the "Son of Man" who according to Daniel 7:13 was to come in the clouds of heaven. For some strange reason the most common self-designation of Jesus in the Gospels ("Son of man") drops out and is not used elsewhere in the New Testament (Acts 7:56 is the one clear exception). We know, however, that Christ is meant when Paul speaks of waiting for the Son from heaven. Some Christians unfortunately are waiting for "events" to happen, but in the New Testament the person of the Savior overshadows all our hopes for the future.

And the ground for our hope of Christ's return is the fact that God raised him from the dead. He was the firstfruits, as Paul puts it in 1 Corinthians 15:23, and because he lives we shall live also. As God raised Jesus by his power, so will he raise us up in his good time (1 Cor. 6:14). The risen Lord who ascended into the heavens will return in due time.

His coming does not strike fear into the hearts of the believers for the risen Christ "rescues us from the coming wrath." God's wrath is not to be understood as bad temper,

irrascibility, spite, malice and the like. Rather, his wrath is God's response to all wickedness. That in no way contradicts the fact that he is love. God loves the sinner to the limit; he sacrificed his Son for our fallen human race. But when people persist in rebellion against God they experience his wrath.

God's wrath is already revealed from heaven, says Paul (Rom. 1:18), but in our text he looks at the final day of judgment, the day of wrath and the revelation of the righteous judgment (Rom. 2:5). Verses like this should correct all sentimental views of God. We do not presume to know the mysteries of the wrath of God and it is not a doctrine that is pleasant to bear. If, however, we want to remain true to the gospel, we cannot avoid this solemn truth that some day God will judge the ungodly.

Personal Response

1. *If the doctrine of election is a way of teaching us that our salvation is by grace alone, should we then be so tentative about it?*
2. *How does God give us the assurance of salvation? (See v. 5).*
3. *How does disreputable behavior on the part of Christians affect the witness of the church in the community?*
4. *What would it mean in our day to "imitate" Christ and the apostles?*
5. *What contribution does v. 6 make to our understanding of Christian joy?*
6. *What might be some of the idols we need to be freed from?*

CHAPTER THREE

IN THE SERVICE OF CHRIST

You know, brothers, that our visit to you was not a failure. We had previously suffered and been insulted in Philippi, as you know, but with the help of our God we dared to tell you his gospel in spite of strong opposition. For the appeal we make does not spring from error or impure motives, nor are we trying to trick you. On the contrary, we speak as men approved by God to be entrusted with the gospel. We are not trying to please men but God, who tests our hearts. You know we never used flattery, nor did we put on a mask to cover up greed—God is our witness. We were not looking for praise from men, not from you or anyone else.

As apostles of Christ we could have been a burden to you, but we were gentle among you, like a mother caring for her little children. We loved you so much that we were delighted to share with you not only the gospel of God but our lives as well, because you had become so dear to us. Surely you remember, brothers, our toil and hardship; we worked night and day in order not to be a burden to anyone while we preached the gospel of God to you.

You are witnesses, and so is God, of how holy, righteous and blameless we were among you who believed. For you know that we dealt with each of you as a father deals with his own children, encouraging, comforting and urging you to live lives worthy of God, who calls you into his kingdom and glory (1 Thess. 2:1-12).

In chapter 1 Paul recalls the marvellous grace of God that came to the Thessalonians through the coming of the gospel. Whenever he thinks of his converts in Thessalonica he thanks God for the miracle of the new life in Christ that took place in that city. Paul continues to reminisce on the experiences he and his colleagues had when they came to plant a church in Thessalonica. Whereas chapter 1 focuses on the Thessalonians, our text is concerned with the experiences of the missionaries when they came to Thessalonica, lived and worked among the people, and modelled for their converts true service for Christ. Although the text is autobiographical it is at the same time parenetic, for indirectly Paul is encouraging his readers to follow the example of the missionaries.

For us who are far removed from the first century context of this letter, there is much that we can learn from this passage in terms of motivation and manner and method as we seek to serve Christ in the twentieth century.

I. Courage in Service (vv. 1,2).

By speaking once again of the "entrance" the apostles had had in Thessalonica, Paul links this passage with 1:5 where Paul mentions their reception by the Thessalonians. Here he adds that their "entrance" had not been in vain. Literally the word *kenos* (in vain) means "empty." Some have read that word to mean that the missionaries did not come "empty handed," that is, they had something to bring. They came in the fullness of the gospel.

More likely the word *kenos* has to do with the results of their mission: it was not in vain; God gave them much fruit for their labor. Assuming that that is the correct meaning, it is a rather unpretentious way of speaking of a very successful missionary venture, and is a gentle reminder for us not to overstate our successes in the work of the kingdom of God. The perfect tense of the verb "was" in Greek suggests that the results of their labors can still be felt; they are abiding.

Repeatedly in this passage Paul will refresh the memory of his readers and our passage, too, begins with "You yourselves know." Since they were eye-witnesses of the mission efforts of the apostles, they will have no difficulty in endorsing what Paul has to say about those early days of the church in Thessalonica.

The readers no doubt knew, also, that Paul and Silas had suffered terribly in Philippi before they came to Thessalonica. They were beaten and imprisoned and treated shamelessly—especially when one considers that they were Roman citizens. The verb *hubrizo* means that they were shamefully treated; they had been publicly stripped and flogged without even an inquiry, and then incarcerated.

Why does Paul mention this tragic experience that preceded their coming to Thessalonica? Certainly not to solicit sympathy but rather to underscore the integrity of the missionaries. If they had been in this work for personal gain they certainly would not have left one place of torment and made themselves vulnerable once again in the next city. One can read between lines here and tell that the enemies of the church were spreading evil rumors about the missionaries. Paul feels le   .d the sincerity of their efforts in preaching t'

To p   .cerated backs into a new city and begin to preach   the Jewish synagogue, from which they could expect .o be expelled, took courage. And the apostles had courage. The verb *parresiazomai* means just that. It refers to open and fearless speech. In Greek democracy it referred to the freedom of speech that citizens prided themselves on. But in a conflict situation, as in our text, it means to be daring, courageous, bold.

This courage, however, was not simply a mark of physical strength and inner fortitude; they had this courage from God. It took more than toughness of character to speak the gospel of God when the opposition to this message was so strong. The word *agon* (from which we derive "agony") suggests that there were opposing forces; it was a word used to describe athletic and even military contests. Although the word could also point to the inner struggles the apostles must have had when they pioneered in Thessalonica, it probably has to do more with external opposition to their work.

This opposition had in fact not ceased when the missionaries left Thessalonica. The enemies of the gospel were trying now to discredit them. Evidently they had launched a smear campaign. They tried to picture the apostles as charlatans, fly-by-night tramps who had come to Thessalonica for personal gain and when the opposition developed they took to their heels. From the defence that Paul makes of his motives in coming to Thessalonica we can gather that some of his readers were tempted to believe this torrent of abuse. And so the apostle will say something on motives in Christian service.

II. Motivation in Service (vv. 3,4).

A. Denial of False Motives.

"For the appeal we make does not spring from error or impure motives, nor are we trying to trick you" (v. 3).

Paul uses the word "appeal" (*paraklesis*) to describe the manner in which the apostles proclaimed God's message. The word has other meanings as well, such as "comfort," or "exhortation." The emphasis seems to lie not so much on the content of their message as on the wooing manner in which they presented it. They not only taught their hearers the historical facts of the Christ event, but they also urged them to accept the good news, and they did this not in a brusque but in a winsome manner.

Their appeal did not spring from error, from deceit. Paul and his associates did of course not teach lies. However, the word "error" may also be a reference to the tricky manner in which a speaker might seek to convince his hearers. In just a moment Paul will deny having used flattery. Paul did not think that the end justified the means and so he and his colleagues not only taught the truth as it is in Jesus but they also rejected deceitful methods in winning people for the faith.

Another motive that he denies is that of "impurity." That could be understood to be a reference to sexual faults— something not uncommon among wandering teachers in Paul's day. One can only imagine how a charge of sexual misdemeanors would have shaken the faith of these young Christians, if it could be made to stick. Perhaps its better to take "impurity" to refer to impure motives, such as pride, greed, and ambition. He will mention some of these evil motives in verses 5 and 6.

Moreover, Paul denies that they used trickery in their work of evangelism. The word "trickery" (*dolos*) quite literally means "bait." All craftiness and subterfuge is unworthy of servants of Christ and the apostles rejected the use of devious methods in their ministry.

B. The Desire for Pure Motives.

"On the contrary, we speak as men approved by God to be entrusted with the gospel. We are not trying to please men but God, who tests our hearts"(v. 4).

The verb *dokimazo* can mean "to put to the test, examine" and then, as the result of the test, to approve. God had tested Paul and found him trustworthy. Precisely what Paul has in mind is hard to determine. He claims (Gal. 1:15) that God had his eye on him even before he was born. When God called him to be his servant he told Paul that he was a "chosen vessel." To Timothy he writes that God considered him trustworthy "appointing me to his service" (I Tim. 1:12).

Whether the approval of which Paul speaks here refers to his pre-Christian life or his post-conversion experience is not clear, but one matter is beyond dispute; he had been entrusted with the gospel. The passive voice suggests that God had entrusted him with the good news of redemption. A stewardship was entrusted to Paul (I Cor. 9:17). At times this realization overwhelmed the apostle. "To me the least of all saints is given this grace to preach to the Gentiles the unsearchable riches of Christ" (Eph. 3:8).

We should notice here the derivative nature of the gospel. Paul did not invent it or create it; it was given to him. Some aspects of the gospel were handed down to him by other apostles, others were given to him by revelation. The gospel can be proclaimed in an infinite variety of ways, but we cannot re-create or change the gospel; that is a given, a sacred trust.

And because God had entrusted the gospel to Paul and his co-workers, they seek to please God rather than people. This desire does not stand in contradiction to 1 Corinthians 10:33 where Paul contends that he does in fact try to please people "in order that they may be saved." The apostles tried to avoid offending people by their manner of life; they befriended people in order to win them for the gospel. But that is not the same as "playing up" to people. The missionaries were concerned that God was pleased with their efforts; they were not in a popularity contest.

Since it was their ultimate desire to please God, their lives were always open to divine scrutiny. God constantly tests their hearts. The heart, in Hebraic thought, is the centre of our personality. What a person is in the heart is what he or she really is. Heart stands for thought, and feeling, and willing. That God examines the inner recesses of the human heart is often stated in the Old Testament (e.g. Jer. 17:10; Ps. 139:23). One of the names for God in Greek is *kardiognostes* (Acts 1:24). He is indeed a "heart specialist." If we live our lives openly before God, under his scrutiny, we will also want to please him, and that is the highest goal that we can aspire to.

II. Nobility in Service (vv. 5-8).

A. Sincere in Motives (vv. 5,6).

The apostle expresses his concern for sincere motives in Christian service negatively, by denying four unworthy motives which the missionaries evidently were accused of. First of all, he denies ever having used flattery. Verbal flattery is not worthy of the nobility of Christian ministry. Flattery must not be confused with words of affirmation or praise. Paul paid some people high compliments. But that is quite different from dishonest speech by which one hopes to exploit people for one's own ends.

Secondly, Paul denies greed as a motive in the ministry of the missionaries. "Nor did we put on a mask to cover up greed." The apostles did not pretend to be interested in their converts when in fact they were interested in material gain. The word "greed" (*leonexia*) literally means "the desire to have more." Covetousness was idolatry in the eyes of Paul (Eph. 5:5). Sometimes the word is used in a wider sense for sinful desires, but here it seems to be limited to monetary avarice. In this particular matter he calls on God as his witness. Appealing to God as his witness has an Old Testament background (Job 16:19; Ps. 89:37), and seems singularly appropriate when inner motives are in question, since no human being can look into another person's heart—only God can.

Thirdly, the missionaries did not come to Thessalonica to receive human praise. "We were not looking for praise from men, not from you or anyone else"(v. 6). The temptation to elicit praise and compliments from others is a well-known temptation for those who work in the eyes of the public. Paul encourages his converts to "honor" Christ's servants (cf. Phil. 2:29), but that is not the same as "seeking" glory (*doxa* in the Greek). There is no suggestion here that the Thessalonians had failed in honoring God's messenger, but Paul simply affirms that they had not demanded honor from them.

Not only had the missionaries been sincere in their motivation, but they had also been gentle in manner.

B. Gentle in Manner (vv. 7,8).

"As apostles of Christ we could have been a burden to you, but we were gentle among you, like a mother caring for her little children" (v. 7).

Whether Paul meant to include Timothy in the rank of the apostles here is not quite clear. Silas very likely had seen the risen Christ. Perhaps the "we" is the polite literary plural.

As Christ's messengers they might have insisted on their authority, their dignity, perhaps even on financial support. Both Jesus and Paul taught that a laborer was worthy of his hire (Luke 10:7; 1 Cor. 9:3-18), but this was a pioneer situation and the missionaries could not risk making a wrong impression upon the Thessalonians. In any case, they did not make it hard for those whom they sought to win for Christ.

We have a manuscript discrepancy in the Greek text in verse 7. Some manuscripts and versions read *epioi* (gentle) and others read *nepioi* (babes). The question now is, what did Paul say originally, "gentle" or "babes?" Usually when Paul uses the picture of "babes" he uses it in a pejorative sense, for immaturity. In just a moment he will compare himself to a nursing mother and then to a father, and so it would seem rather strange that he should also compare himself and his colleagues with babes. If that should be the correct meaning then we would have to think of the missionaries as being "like children among children."

However, although the manuscript evidence is not as strong for the reading "gentle," that seems to fit the context better. The picture of a mother tenderly caring for her child would then be an elaboration of this gentleness which characterized the apostles. As a nursing mother fondles and cuddles her baby, so Paul and his colleagues had cared tenderly for the Thessalonians.

He goes on to say that "we loved you so much that we were delighted to share with you not only the gospel of God, but our lives as well, because you had become so dear to us"(v. 8). It may surprise us to find such words of endearment coming from a tough and muscular man such as Paul must have been, but it is the kind of language those who are in leadership and who tend to become autocratic need to hear. The apostles served "with yearning love" (NEB), not in a cold-blooded, professional manner.

Just what Paul means when he says that they had been willing to share their lives with the Thessalonians is not altogether clear. It could mean that they were willing to lay down their lives for their converts. And certainly it would include sharing some of the experiences of their lives, their conversion, for example. But in the context we should probably think of "sharing" in the sense of entering into the lives of the Thessalonians—giving freely of their time, their energy, their compassion, rejoicing with the joyful and weeping with the sorrowful. They simply put their lives at the disposal of the people whom they were seeking to win and establish in the faith.

C. Diaconic in Spirit (v. 9a).

"Surely you remember, brothers, our toil and hardship; we worked night and day in order not to be a burden to anyone."

Paul assumes that the readers remember how hard the apostles had worked when they were with them in order not to be a burden to the Thessalonians. They displayed a diaconic spirit, a servant attitude. And they demonstrated this by supporting themselves with the labor of their own hands. It's hard to translate the word-play *kopos kai mochthos* (toil and moil) which describes the hardship and the fatigue that the missionaries had taken upon themselves in order to win the Thessalonians. When Paul says they worked "night and day" he doesn't mean that they never rested, but sometimes they worked also at night in order to support themselves. (The order "night and day" is typically the Hebrew way of speaking; we might say "from dawn to dusk.") The self-supporting ministry has much to be said for it and, in any case, has good biblical precedent.

IV. Methods of Service (vv. 9b-12).

A. Proclamation.

"We preached the gospel of God to you" (v. 9).

It may well be that they preached at night and labored during the day at some trade. Paul had learned to work with leather as a tent-maker. The Philippian church had sent some monetary support to Paul while he worked in Thessalonica but that evidently had not been sufficient for room and board. The word Paul uses for preaching here is *kerusso* (a *kerux* was a town crier, a herald) and means to announce, to proclaim. Whether they did this in the open air, or in the synagogue, or in a rented hall (as in Ephesus), or even while they were working at their trade, is not stated. But what they did proclaim was the "good news of God," that is, good news about God, but also the good news from God, that God in Christ had reconciled the world to himself.

B. Presence (v. 10).

"You are witnesses, and so is God, of how holy, righteous and blameless we were among you who believed." The proclamation of the gospel was supported by the godly life of the messengers. Again Paul needs only to refresh their memories, for they had observed the apostles with their own eyes.

Three adverbs describe the life of the missionaries. "Holy" suggests that they lived a life devoted God. There was a reverence for God in their lives that expressed itself in genuine piety. "Righteous" may point rather more in a manward direction, in contrast to "holy" which points godward. However, these terms should not be distinguished too neatly. "Blameless" means to live without fault in the eyes of God and people. The people he has in mind here are the Thessalonians ("among you who believe").

C. Pastoral Care (vv. 11,12).

"For you know that we dealt with each of you as a father deals with his own children, encouraging, comforting and urging you to live lives worthy of God, who calls you into his kingdom and glory."

Earlier he used the picture of motherhood to describe the manner in which the apostles dealt with their converts. Now the metaphor changes and he describes the missionaries in their fatherly role, seeking to educate, to shape and to form the lives of these young believers.

The missionaries paid individual attention to each of their converts ("we dealt with each one of you"). They exhorted these young Christians, encouraged them, and urged them strongly to live lives that are worthy of God. The Philippians are urged to walk worthy of the gospel (1:27); the Ephesians are exhorted to walk worthy of their calling (4:1); and the Thessalonians are asked to walk worthy of God.

"To walk" is one of the most common metaphors for a person's way of life. Christians were, among other things, called "people of the way" (Acts 9:2). Like the saints of the Old Testament they are called to live holy lives because God is holy (Lev. 11:45). And this God keeps on calling his children into his eternal kingdom. God's kingdom, his reign, broke into this world with the coming of Jesus, but there is yet a future dimension to this kingdom, when it comes in all its glory.

Personal Response

1. What motivates us in our service for Christ?
2. Is there a place today for self-supporting ministries?
3. What light does our passage cast on "friendship" evangelism?
4. What does it mean to "walk worthy of God"?
5. How does God keep on calling us into his kingdom and his glory?

CHAPTER FOUR

CHURCH PLANTING, FIRST CENTURY STYLE

And we also thank God continually because, when you received the word of God, which you heard from us, you accepted it not as the word of men, but as it actually is, the word of God, which is at work in you who believe. For you, brothers, became imitators of God's churches in Judea, which are in Christ Jesus: You suffered from your own countrymen the same things those churches suffered from the Jews, who killed the Lord Jesus and the prophets and also drove us out. They displease God and are hostile to all men in their effort to keep us from speaking to the Gentiles so that they may be saved. In this way they always heap up their sins to the limit. The wrath of God has come upon them at last.

But, brothers, when we were torn away from you for a short time (in person, not in thought), out of our intense longing we made every effort to see you. For we wanted to come to you—certainly I, Paul, did, again and again—but Satan stopped us. For what is our hope, our joy, or the crown in which we will glory in the presence of our Lord Jesus when he comes? Is it not you? Indeed, you are our glory and joy.

So when we could stand it no longer, we thought it best to be left by ourselves in Athens. We sent Timothy, who is our brother and God's fellow worker in spreading the gospel of Christ, to strengthen and encourage you in your faith, so that no one would be unsettled by these trials. You know quite well that we were destined for them. In fact, when we were with you, we kept telling you that we would be persecuted. And it turned out that way, as you well know. For this reason, when I could stand it no longer, I sent to find out about your faith. I was afraid that in some way the tempter might have tempted you and our efforts might have been useless.

But Timothy has just now come to us from you and has brought good news about your faith and love. He has told us that you always have pleasant memories of us and that you long to see us, just as we also long to see you. Therefore, brothers, in all our distress and persecution we were encouraged about you because of your faith. For now we really live, since you are standing firm in the Lord. How can we thank God enough for you in return for all the joy we have in the presence of our God because of you? Night and day we pray most earnestly that we may see you again and supply what is lacking in your faith.

Now may our God and Father himself and our Lord Jesus clear the way for us to come to you. May the Lord make your love increase and overflow for each other and for everyone else, just as ours does for you. May he strengthen your hearts so that you will be blameless and holy in the presence of our God and Father when our Lord Jesus comes with all his holy ones (1 Thess. 2:13-3:13).

We do not know precisely how long Paul and his coworkers worked in Thessalonica. Their ministry was abruptly terminated when the unbelieving Jews in the city instigated a riot and dragged Jason, Paul's host, before the authorities, who took bail from him. Under cover of darkness Paul and Silas left the city and moved on to Beroea. However, Thessalonian Jews harassed the missionaries here as well, and so, leaving Silas and Timothy behind, Paul came to Athens.

Some of Paul's converts may have been tempted to think "out of sight, out of mind," and evidently the enemies of the Christian faith were spreading the rumor that Paul was a "fly-by-night" missionary who cared little for his converts and could not be trusted. In the following paragraphs Paul will show that there is no foundation to such calumny and that, in fact, his friendship for them is deep and strong. Circumstances, however, had not allowed him to come back to them. Our passage begins with a review of the early days when the gospel came to Thessalonica. This is followed by an explanation for Paul's absence and expressions of his continued concern for their spiritual welfare. The entire passage closes with a prayer for the Thessalonians. The passage gives us some delightful insights into how churches were planted in the first century.

I. Founding the Church (2:13-16).

A. Receiving the Word of God (v. 13).

Paul picks up the note of thanksgiving with which he opened his letter (1:2). Paul remembers vividly bringing the gospel to Thessalonica, and how many of his hearers responded to the gospel by accepting it. He can never recall that experience without breaking into thanksgiving.

When the Thessalonians heard the gospel they received it as God's word and not simply as a human message. Of course, Paul's voice was human, he operated with his own Greek vocabulary, used his own illustrations. But those very human words were used by God to convey the message of salvation. The gospel is not simply a digest of human opinions, wishes and hopes, but it is God's message offering salvation to those who receive it.

Once the message has been received it continues to work in the lives of believers. The verb *energeo* (work) suggests that a supernatural power continues to transform the believers, making them more and more Christlike.

B. Suffering for the Faith (vv. 14-16).

The acceptance of the gospel brought not only the assurance of forgiveness of sins and acceptance by God, but it also brought with it persecution. In that respect they became "imitators of God's churches in Judea, which are in Christ Jesus." The writers of the New Testament can speak of "the church" in Judea (Acts 9:31) as well as of "the churches" in Judea. Paul is careful to add that the churches in Judea he has in mind belong to God; they do not belong to the founder or the leader. However, since Jewish synagogues would also claim to belong to God, Paul is even more explicit and says that they are "in Christ Jesus."

In 1:6 he commended the Thessalonians for becoming imitators of the apostles and of the Lord. That was a voluntary, deliberate decision on the part of the readers. But to become imitators of persecuted churches was not something they sought; it was forced upon them by the enemies of the gospel. What happened earlier to Judean churches happened also to the Thessalonians. Why Paul singled out the suffering of the Judean churches is hard to say. Could it be that he still had vivid memories of how he himself persecuted the believers in Judea? The cross, of course, had pulled the sting out of that memory, but he always remembered this awful mistake he made when he was an unbeliever.

Who the "countrymen" are who persecuted the Thessalonian believers is not stated, but it would probably include both unbelieving Jews and Gentiles. The Judean churches, however, had suffered at the hands of the Jews, and that leads Paul to speak some harsh words about his own countrymen who caused the church so much grief in the early years of its history. There is no doubt about Paul's love for his people, and we should view verses 15 and 16 as outburst coming from the heart of an exasperated missionary. The six charges that he makes against Jewish countrymen were, of course, only too true.

One, they killed the Lord Jesus. Actually the Romans did the killing but the Jewish leaders forced Pilate's hand after the Sanhedrin had condemned him to death. That doesn't mean that we should hold the Jewish people as a whole responsible for Jesus' death, but the apostles put the blame for the death of our Lord at the feet of the Jewish hierarchy (Acts 2:23,36; 3:13-17).

Two, they killed the prophets. The deaths of Old Testament prophets are largely undocumented in the Old Testament, but Jewish traditions about the martyrdom of several Old Testament prophets are well-known. Jesus himself confirmed that his contemporaries were descendants of those "who murdered the prophets" (Mt. 23:31).

Three, they drove out the apostles. This is very likely a reference to the experience of the missionaries at Thessalonica, for they slipped away to Beroea, in order to not endanger the lives of their converts.

Four, they displeasd God. To please God means to take seriously his commandments and to live in obedience to the norm of behavior that God has set forth in his word. In 2:4 Paul speaks of his sincere desire to please God. God certainly was displeased with the Jewish resistance to the gospel.

Five, they oppose all people. That's the kind of judgment one can find also in contemporary Roman writers such as Tacitus. Paul, however, is not an anti-Semitist, for he has the hostility which the unbelieving Jews have shown to the messengers of the gospel in mind. One should read Romans 9:1-5 along with our text to feel the deep love that Paul had for his people.

Six, they "keep us from speaking to the Gentiles so that they may be saved" (v. 16a). Not only did they try to stop Paul's attempt to bring the gospel to Jews, but also to Gentiles. The Book of Acts gives a number of illustrations of how unbelieving Jews tried to interfere in Paul's mission to the Gentiles (Acts 13:45-50; 14:2,19; 17:5-9; 18:12). It should be noted, also, that Paul firmly believed that it was through the witness of the gospel that people were saved. Although it is not stated from what the Gentiles were saved, we must assume that it is deliverance from the power of sin and death that Paul had in mind.

As a result of this resistance to the gospel "they always heap up their sins to the limit" (v. 16b). The metaphor is that of a cup filled to the brim. It is said of the Amorites (Gen. 15:16) and of the Pharisees (Matt. 23:32) that they had filled up the measure of sins. And because of this "the wrath of God has come upon them at last" (v. 16c). Perhaps the many troubles that were breaking out all over the empire in Paul's day were for him a sign that the judgment of God was about to strike apostate Judaism. God's wrath was hanging over their heads and when God's hour would strike it would engulf the Jewish people.

Fortunately this is not the entire picture of Judaism, as far as Paul is concerned. Although he has stated a number of bald facts, he never gave up on his people, and in Romans 9-11 he expresses the hope that the branches of the Abrahamic tree that have been broken off because of unbelief, will some day be re-ingrafted. In fact Paul continued to speak to synagogue audiences whenever he could and even when he came to Rome as prisoner he met with the Jewish leaders to "declare to them the kingdom of God" (Acts 28:16-31).

II. Worrying About the Church (2:17-3:5).

After this brief review of how the Thessalonians received the gospel in the face of so much opposition, Paul explains his absence to his readers. Evidently there were critics who thought Paul was an irresponsible charlatan who was out for personal gain. His percipitate departure could not be explained any other way, they thought. And so the apostle explains why he had left so suddenly and why he had not come back to see them. The entire paragraph expresses his deep concern about the welfare of these young converts, and so one might justly speak of worrying about them. The word "worry" is sometimes used in a pejorative sense (cf. Phil. 4:6), but we are using it here in the sense of pastoral care.

A. The Forced Absence (2:17-20).

"But, brothers, when we were torn away from you for a short time (in person, not in thought), out of our intense longing we made every effort to see you" (v. 17). *Aporphanizo* means quite literally "leave as orphans," and by usage means deprivation or desolation. The apostles were torn away from this infant church by their forcible expulsion from Thessalonica. Paul is hopeful that his separation from them is temporary ("for the space of an hour"), and in any case it is only a bodily absence, not an absence of heart and mind. Their thoughts were with the Thessalonians constantly, and they even tried desperately to see their face again.

For this reason Paul tried again and again to come to them but Satan stopped him and his associates (v. 18). Just how Satan had "cut in" on them when they wanted to return to Thessalonica is not stated. Nor does Paul explain how he knew that it was indeed Satan who had prevented them from returning. We know, too, that upon occasion the Spirit of Jesus prevented Paul from carrying out his plans (cf. Acts 16:6,7). Perhaps Paul was certain that in this instance Satan had prevented them from carrying out their plans because no good purpose was served by putting obstacles in their way, whereas when God prevented him from carrying out his plans he could see in retrospect that they had led to the furtherance of the gospel. In any case, Paul's absence was not due to indifference on his part.

Paul now becomes almost lyrical in his expressions of affection for the Thessalonians. This letter has been called a classic of friendship. "For what is our hope, our joy, or the crown in which we will glory in the presence of our Lord Jesus when he comes? Is it not you? Indeed, you are our glory and joy" (vv. 19,20). Paul had feared (3:5) that the adversary might have tempted them to abandon their new-found faith, but now that Timothy has come with a good report he is full of hope.

Also, they are a source of joy for Paul. It's a bit like a

parent saying of his or her child, "You are the joy of my heart." However, it should be noted that Paul has the coming of Christ in mind, and on that day his hope for the Thessalonians will be fulfilled, his joy will be full, and they will be a "crown of boasting" for him. On the last day the Thessalonians will be like a victory wreath that will be placed on the apostle's head.

The Greek word for Christ's coming at the end of the age is *parousia*—a word found six times in the two Thessalonian letters. Literally the word means "presence." Also, it is used to describe the "arrival" of a person. However, it had acquired a more technical meaning in New Testament times and was used for the arrival, the visit, of the emperor or some other dignitary. The writers of the New Testament take that word and carry it over to the glorious appearance of the great God and Savior, Jesus Christ, at the end of the age.

B. The Friendly Visit (3:1-5).

After explaining to his readers why he had not come back to Thessalonica, and showering them with expressions of love and affection, he fills them in on what efforts he had, in fact, made to contact them. Since the apostles had been harassed by Thessalonian Jews in Beroea just as they had been in Thessalonica, Paul left for Athens. Who else accompanied him besides Timothy is not stated. However, while in Athens Paul felt the separation from the Thessalonians so keenly that he could hardly stand it any longer. And since Paul himself could not return to Thessalonica he was willing to be abandoned in Athens and to send Timothy back to see how the church was faring. He was willing to endure loneliness rather than to live in suspense over his converts in Thessalonica.

Timothy is described here as "our brother and God's fellow worker in spreading the gospel of Christ" (3:2). Some copyists of the New Testament manuscripts were taken aback by this rather exalted position of Timothy (God's fellow worker) and introduced all kinds of alternate readings. Some manuscripts have "servant" instead of fellow worker, others have both terms, and still others omit the word "God," making Timothy a fellow worker of Paul. But clearly these are attempts to water down the expression "God's fellow worker" (cf. 1 Cor. 3:9 for a parallel).

The immediate purpose of sending Timothy back to Thessalonica was to "strengthen" and to "encourage" his converts in the faith. These verbs are found frequently in the parenetic (hortatory) passages of the New Testament. Timothy was to strengthen these young believers lest they be shaken in their faith by the trials they had to face. One way in which to strengthen was to explain to the Thessalonians that suffering was a part of a Christian's life here on earth. "You know quite well that we were destined for them" (3:3b). Implied is that they had been told this when the missionaries were with them, but they needed to be reminded of the fact that suffering is part and parcel of the Christian way of life. "We must go through many hardships to enter the kingdom of God," said Paul to his converts in Antioch of Pisidia (Acts 14:22). For this reason one finds it exceedingly strange to be told by some popular preachers in our day that if we follow Jesus we are assured of health and wealth.

Not only did Paul want to strengthen the Thessalonians through the visit of Timothy, but he also wanted to find out about their faith. Faith here is a comprehensive term for the Christian state. Although Paul had full confidence in the power of God to keep the believers safe, he had no illusions about the power of the "tempter," Satan. The word "to tempt" can mean either to put to the test or to seduce. God tests his children, but he never seduces them. Satan is out to deceive them and to induce them to deny their faith. Clearly, then, the apostle was conscious of a spiritual warfare that is carried on in higher realms between God and Satan. Should the Thessalonians fall away from the faith, the work of the missionaries would have been in vain.

III. Enjoying the Church (3:6-10)

After reminding his readers of the wonderful days when they came to know Christ, and explaining his unavoidable absence and his worries about them, Paul can now relax and enjoy the Thessalonian readers. Timothy has returned from Thessalonica and brought a positive report. Paul is, however, no longer in Athens but in Corinth, and it was in Corinth that he heard the good news about the church.

A. Occasion for Rejoicing (3:6).

"But Timothy has just now come to us from you, and has brought good news about your faith and love" (v. 6a). Paul calls Timothy's report a "gospel" (*euangelizomai* is elsewhere used for "preaching the gospel"). Here we see again how the apostles take current secular vocabulary (as found in our text) and fill it with new meaning (when the verb refers to the proclamation of the good news of redemption in Christ).

"Faith and love" are here a kind of comprehensive word-pair for their Christian life. We have already had the familiar trilogy of "faith, love and hope" (1:3). Also, Timothy has reported that the Thessalonians have pleasant memories of the apostles and that they long to see them (3:6b). It is no small mercy when a congregation remembers its ministers with affection. How sad when a church is secretly glad to see a pastor leave!

B. The Expressions of Joy (3:7-10).

So overwhelmed was Paul by the good news brought by Timothy that he felt encouraged and comforted (*parakaleo* can mean both) in the midst of his distress and affliction. Establishing a church in Corinth was no easy task and so a good report about the faith of the Thessalonians was a tonic for Paul's soul. Now he felt like living again; he could breathe again. Timothy's report gave him strength to carry on in the face of much opposition.

Somewhat rhetorically Paul asks, "How can we thank God enough for you in return for all the joy we have in the presence of our God because of you?" (v.9). Somehow Paul feels that his thanks to God is cold and inadequate when compared with the joy that is his when he thinks of the Thessalonian church. One is reminded of the words of the Psalmist, "What shall I render to the Lord for all his bounty to me?" (Ps. 116:12).

Paul's joy is, however, tempered with the recognition that the young church still has needs. They are still in danger, and they are still far from perfect. And so Paul adds a prayer to his thanksgiving that God might open the way for them so that they might come to Thessalonica. "Night and day we pray most earnestly that we may see you again" (v.10a). Paul is confident that the hindrances which Satan had put in their way till now can be removed. When in God's own time Paul will visit them he will not only enjoy their presence ("see their face"), but he will also want to supply what is lacking in their faith (v.10b). No doubt there were gaps not only in their doctrinal understanding but also in their ethical behavior, and Paul would love to lead them on to higher ground.

IV. Praying for the Church (3:11-13).

Since he cannot visit the Thessalonians at the moment he does what he can for them: he remembers them in prayer.

A. The Address (v. 11a).

"Now may our God and Father himself and our Lord Jesus." In the process of writing this letter Paul breaks out in prayer and then incorporates this prayer into his letter, as he frequently does. He addresses his petitions to God the

Father and the Lord Jesus. God and Jesus are coupled in such a way that we have to assume that for Paul Jesus is divine. The title "Lord" would also underscore that. And the fact that God revealed himself as our Father in the coming of Jesus. "Anyone who has seen me has seen the Father" (John 14:9).

B. The Petitions (vv. 11b-13).

Paul makes three requests when he prays: One, he prays that the way be cleared so that he could come to them (v. 11b). Paul is sure that God can "make straight" (*kateuthuno*) the way which Satan had blocked (2:18). This prayer was answered but, as it seems, only several years later.

Two, he prays that the Lord will make their love to increase and to overflow toward one another (v. 12). The two verbs "increase" and "overflow" are hendiadys, that is, two words used as one for emphasis. Paul not only acknowledges the presence of love in the church (cf. 1:3; 4:9), but maintains that unlimited growth in love is possible. "To one another and to all" would suggest that their love embrace not only the members of the church but reach out to those who are not yet believers. Often it is through the love of a Christian that unbelievers are won for the faith. And what Paul asks of his converts he models in his own life, "just as we do to you."

Three, he prays: "May God strengthen your hearts so that you will be blameless and holy in the presence of our God and Father when our Lord Jesus comes with all his holy ones" (v. 13).

As they grow in love their hearts will be established in holiness. The heart stands for the whole inner being. To establish the heart means to consolidate and build up the entire inner life. There is an initial sanctification of the person that takes place at conversion, but here Paul has the ongoing process of sanctification in mind. He wants them to be blameless in holiness before God the Father when our Lord Jesus comes in his *parousia*. At this *parousia* he will be accompanied by "all his holy ones." That could mean "angels" but could also refer to the "saints." Perhaps it's best to include both. And, as we might expect, Paul concludes his prayer with an "Amen!"

Personal Response

1. *How can words spoken by human beings be the word of God (2:13)?*
2. *Is Paul's denunciation of apostate Judaism (2:15,16) more severe than that of the Old Testament prophets or of Jesus? (cf. Mt. 23).*
3. *Can we ascribe every frustration in our efforts to build the kingdom of God to Satan? (cf. 2:18)*
4. *What kind of trials did Paul have in mind when he said we were destined for them (3:3)?*
5. *In what sense does Paul's prayer in 3:11 encourage us to pray for God's help in the everyday affairs of life?*

CHAPTER FIVE

PLEASING GOD IN EVERYDAY LIFE

> *Finally, brothers, we instructed you how to live in order to please God, as in fact you are living. Now we ask you and urge you in the Lord Jesus to do this more and more. For you know what instructions we gave you by the authority of the Lord Jesus.*
>
> *It is God's will that you should be sanctified; that you should avoid sexual immorality; that each of you should learn to control his own body in a way that is holy and honorable, not in passionate lust like the heathen, who do not know God; and that in this matter no one should wrong his brother or take advantage of him. The Lord will punish men for all such sins, as we have already told you and warned you. For God did not call us to be impure, but to live a holy life. Therefore, he who rejects this instruction does not reject man but God, who gives you his Holy Spirit.*
>
> *Now about brotherly love we do not need to write to you, for you yourselves have been taught by God to love each other. And in fact, you do love all the brothers throughout Macedonia. Yet we urge you, brothers, to do so more and more.*
>
> *Make it your ambition to lead a quiet life, to mind your own business and to work with your hands, just as we told you, so that your daily life may win the respect of outsiders and so that you will not be dependent on anybody (1 Thess. 4:1-12).*

With chapter 4 the narrative section of this letter comes to an end and Paul begins to address questions of Christian ethics. Much of what we have in the previous chapters was a review of the founding of the church and Paul's relationship to the believers in Thessalonica. Chapter 4 begins with the word "finally," which, however, may just as well be translated as "furthermore," since we are only at the midpoint of the letter.

The previous chapter closed with a forward look to the *parousia* of our Lord when Paul expects to meet his Thessalonian friends in glory and to rejoice in their presence. Before chapter 4 ends Paul will elaborate the topic of Christ's return (vv. 13-18). Sandwiched in between these two mountain peaks when our faith shall be turned into sight, lies a paragraph on Christian ethics. That is not an uncommon connection; the hope of the *parousia* is to motivate God's people to live holy lives.

Our passage begins with an exhortation to please God and that may well serve as the theme for the entire pericope.

After appealing to his readers to live a life pleasing to God, Paul touches upon several areas in which it is of the utmost importance that they do please God. He then goes on to motivate the Thessalonians to make pleasing God their aim, and ends with some practical suggestions on how they might do this.

I. The Appeal to Please God (4:1,2).

A. The Spirit of the Appeal (v. 1).

Paul begins the parenetic section of his letter with two fraternal verbs, used quite synonymously: "we ask you and urge you." Once again he addresses them as "brothers" (which includes the sisters), indicating that they belong to the new family of God and must therefore live in a different manner from the rest of society.

Although the tone of the appeal is gentle, it is given with the authority of Jesus. Paul is conscious of his apostolic calling and speaks in Jesus' name. What he is asking them to do however is not something that he himself has conjured up, but rather he urges them to observe the Christian teachings which they have received. The word *paralambano* (literally "to receive from the side") is a technical term for the reception of the gospel message and the apostolic teachings which go back to Jesus. These apostolic traditions included ethical guidelines for Christians.

The apostle does not want his readers to think that Christian ethics is optional for those who are interested enough to observe them, but he makes ethics obligatory. "It is necessary" implies that the ethical teachings of Jesus, delivered by the apostles, are binding on the followers of Jesus. And when Christians observe these teachings they please God.

Pleasing God is the highest good a believer can strive for. Of the unbelieving Jews Paul says in 2:15 that they do not please God. By contrast it is said of the godly Enoch that before God took him away he had the testimony that he pleased God (Heb. 11:5). Paul himself had one ambition: "to please him whether we are at home in the body or away from it" (2 Cor. 5:9).

As was Paul's custom, he gives credit where credit is due, and thereby demonstrates that he is a master teacher. After exhorting them "to walk and please God," he quickly adds, "as in fact you are doing." However, if pleasing God is the goal of our life, there are unlimited possibilities, and so Paul urges his readers to do so more and more. There is always new territory to conquer in the Christian life.

It is, however, not enough simply to want to please God. We must also know what pleases him. Horatius Bonar writes, "I love my Master and I want to do his bidding; but I must know the rules of his house; love without the law to guide its impulses, would be parent to will-worship; love goes to the law to learn the divine will." And that leads us to ask for the meaning of this appeal to please God.

B. The Meaning of the Appeal (v. 2).

If people are to please God they must be instructed in the things that please him, and that is what the apostles had done: "For you know what instructions we gave you by the authority of the Lord Jesus." "You know" suggests that ethical instruction was part of the missionary activity of Paul and his associates. They not only led people to Christ but they taught them how to follow Christ.

The instructions which had been given to the readers were not simply a list of do's and don't's (although they would not be absent), but included basic guidelines in matters of ethics. Christians who seek to please God need such guidelines but there has to be some flexibility so that individual believers can make responsible decisions.

II. The Areas in Which They Are to Please God (4:3-6a).

After laying down a comprehensive principle of Christian living, to please God, Paul puts his finger on several specific areas in which he wants the Thessalonians to apply this principle.

A. Sexual Morality (v. 3).

"It is God's will that you should be sanctified; that you should avoid sexual immorality."

As a Jew Paul had been brought up to view the will of God as the ultimate guide and motivation for behavior. This will of God had been revealed to Israel (Rom. 2:17). As a Christian Paul is no less concerned about doing God's will and that included the avoidance of sexual immorality.

Among Evangelicals the term "will of God" is often restricted to the matter of guidance with respect to one's calling, and that is a legitimate application of the term. In the New Testament, however, the expression "will of God" is usually found in the context of Christian ethics, in matters of right and wrong.

It is God's will that we should be holy. The word "sanctification" (*hagiasmos*) points to a process, something that goes on throughout the believer's life. One aspect of sanctification is abstinence from *porneia*. *Porneia* includes every kind of unlawful sexual intercourse. We need not infer from this prohibition to avoid sexual immorality that the Thessalonian church had a reputation for sexual irregularities. Rather, Paul wants to prevent his readers from falling back into pagan ways.

Converts from the Jewish synagogue knew well enough that sexual immorality was contrary to the will of God, but those who came out of raw paganism may not have grasped this principle immediately. The Greco-Roman world was plagued by sexual vices of every kind, although there were sensitive non-Christians in Paul's day who would have agreed with his position. Paul was willing to adapt to the cultural practices of his day. However, if these practices were immoral he took an uncompromising stand against them. His call to chastity may have seemed rather radical to some of his readers, for he returns to that subject in a number of his letters. To please God Christians need to practise moderation in all areas of life, but in the matter of sexual immorality they must make a clean break; they must abstain (literally "keep away") from *porneia*.

B. Self-Control (vv. 4,5).

"That each of you should learn to control his own body in a way that is holy and honorable, not in passionate lust like the heathen, who do not know God."

It is not at all certain that the NIV has hit upon the right translation of the Greek text. The RSV has "that each one of you know how to take a wife for himself" (the New RSV has reversed itself in its translation of the word "vessel"). The word "vessel" can mean a thing, a tool, any container or household utensil. Metaphorically it is used also for persons. Paul was a "chosen vessel" (Acts 9:15). Peter says that the woman is "the weaker vessel" (1 Pet. 3:7). We (both men and women) "have this treasure in earthen vessels" (2 Cor. 4: 7).

In the texts just quoted, the meaning is that of "body." Translators from the earliest centuries have had a difficult time with our text. Should they render "vessel" as "body" or as "wife."

The verb "acquire" would favor the translation "wife." In other words, when a believer seeks for a wife and lives with her, he should do so in holiness and honor, that is, with a high regard for his wife. The argument that this translation suggests a low view of womanhood is not sufficiently strong to tilt it in favor of "body."

Assuming the word vessel means "body," we would have to think of the sexual aspect of the body, and the verb "acquire" would then have to be applied equally to both men and women. Either way, Paul wants the believers to exercise self-control. It is a fruit of the Spirit (Gal. 5:22). The only context in which sexual intercourse is legitimate according to the Scriptures is in a monogamous, heterosexual relationship. Intercourse before marriage (fornication), adultery after marriage, or homosexual activity are out of bounds for the believer who seeks to please God.

It is in the matter of self-control that the church sets itself off from the pagan world. "Not in passionate lust like the heathen who do not know God." To be overpowered by sexual desires is not fitting for the believer. Unwholesome sexual passions which drive people to desire what is forbidden are not pleasing to God. The heathen world, by contrast, because it does not know God, allows passion free rein. Although even the Gentiles know about God (Rom. 1), they do not acknowledge him as such and therefore live by different mores. Paul is not suggesting that all Gentiles live immoral lives, but he uses well-known language of the Old Testament, "the nations that know not God" (Jer. 10:25; Ps. 79:6). Whether it's in the matter of acquiring a wife or in the area of bodily desire, believers are not to be ruled by lust.

C. Mutual Relations (v. 6a).

"And that in this matter no one should wrong his brother or take advantage of him."

Here again we have a translation problem. What does the word *pragma* (matter) mean? Some take it to refer to lawsuits and understand Paul to be warning the Thessalonians not to take advantage of their brothers in lawsuits. But that does not seem to fit the context, for he uses the article "this matter," and that suggests the matter he has just been talking about, namely sexual morality.

Luther understood the word *pragma* to refer to business matters. But the singular noun does not seem to have that meaning. Others have suggested that word means something like our English word "affair," that is, a sexual affair.

It would be unchristian to take adavantage of our brothers or sisters in any matter. However, in our passage it looks as if relations between the sexes are in focus. Implied is that there are boundaries in the realm of sexual relations which a believer is not permitted to cross, for in doing so he or she would be taking advantage of one's brother or sister.

III. The Motivation for Pleasing God (vv. 6b-8).

A. The Nature of God (v. 6b).

Paul will give three reasons why the Thessalonians must take his exhortations to sexual purity seriously, and the first is the character of God. "The Lord will punish men for all such sins, as we have already told you and warned you."

The "Lord" could refer either to God or to Christ. Paul frequently ascribes divine functions to Jesus and so whether we think of God or of Christ, the warning remains unchanged; God is an avenger of all the evils Paul has mentioned. Sexual immorality, a life dominated by lust, every kind of human exploitation stands under the judgment of God. While sin brings with it its own nemesis here in life, Paul probably has God's judgment at the end of the age in mind. For those who have sinned and repent of their transgressions there is pardon and forgiveness offered in the gospel, but that's an aspect not discussed by the apostle at this point.

It should not really surprise the readers to hear that God punishes evil, for the apostles had told their converts this when they brought them the gospel. In fact, they had "solemnly testified" to this solemn truth. That Paul struck the note of divine punishment for sin in his preaching can be seen from some of his recorded sermons (cf. Acts 17:31; 22:25).

B. The Call of God (v. 7).

"For God did not call us to be impure, but to live a holy life."

God's call here refers to the call of the gospel, the call out of darkness to his marvellous light. The word "call" suggests that God takes the initiative in our salvation; we love him because he first loved us. Those who respond to the call of God in the gospel are "the called"—one of the titles used for believers in the New Testament.

When God calls us to come to Jesus in faith, he calls us also to a holy life. It would be preposterous to think that God would call us to uncleanness. His call is given in the sphere of holiness. "Be holy, for I am holy," is both an Old Testament as well as a New Testament maxim for the people of God.

However, not only the nature of God and the call of God motivate us to live holy lives, but also the fact that God gives us the Holy Spirit.

C. The Gift of God (v. 8).

"Therefore, he who rejects this instruction does not reject man but God, who gives you his Holy Spirit."

To reject what the apostle has been saying about living a holy life would mean that the readers viewed Paul's words as human opinions. Paul, however, is conscious of speaking in God's name, and so his instructions have to be taken seriously. To reject Jesus' messenger would be like rejecting Jesus himself (Mark 9:37; Luke 10:16; John 5:23).

To think lightly of God's call to holiness is all the more serious because he gives us his Spirit, and that Spirit is holy. Living in sin would "grieve" the Holy Spirit (Eph.4:30). The present tense of the verb "give" seems problematic to some readers. Some scribes in the early centuries in fact changed it to a past tense. The present tense simply stresses that God is the Giver of the Holy Spirit. And those who receive this gift from God must not live impure lives.

Paul then turns from the subject of sexual morality to that of love for fellow-believers and he suggests some practical ways in which Christians can please God.

IV. Practical Ways of Pleasing God (vv. 9-12).

A. Abounding in Love (vv. 9,10).

"Now about brotherly love we do not need to write to you, for you yourselves have been taught by God to love each other. And in fact, you do love all the brothers throughout Macedonia. Yet we urge you, brothers, to do so more and more."

The word for "brotherly love" is *philadelphia*. Although that word was used in secular Greek for the love that brothers and sisters have naturally for one another, here it is applied to the spiritual family of God, the church. Sometimes the ties that bind Christian brothers and sisters together, even though they are not related by blood, are closer than between natural brothers and sisters.

Paul feels no need to write to the Thessalonians about this kind of love because they were taught by God (another compound in Greek, *theodidaktoi*). Does that mean they knew this from the Old Testament or does he mean that all Christians know intuitively that they must love their fellow-Christians? Either way, Paul's readers were doing what they were taught by God. Where Paul can, he gives a word of commendation. They do love all the brothers in Macedonia, but they must not draw the boundary there; they must go beyond that. Love for one's fellow-believers is a clear sign that a person has experienced the love of God in Christ. There is always room for growth in our love for others, and Paul encourages the Thessalonians to let God increase their love.

B. Living Quietly (v. 11a)

"Make it your ambition to lead a quiet life."

Where there is brotherly love a person will want also to do his or her fair share of work. Evidently some of the Thessalonians were withdrawing from daily work, thinking perhaps that the *parousia* might take place at any time. It appears as if feverish excitement in anticipation of Christ's coming had led to the neglect of daily duties, and some members were becoming a burden to others. Perhaps, too, this attitude was bringing the church into disrepute with the neighbors, since the admonition ends with encouragement to win the respect of the outsiders.

The exhortation to live quietly is given in a form that we call an oxymoron. "Make it your ambition" to lead a quiet life, seems incongruous. "Be restless to be at rest"; "be ambitious to be unambitiuous." The word "ambition" is found three times in Paul (here; Rom. 15:20, and 2 Cor. 5:9) and means literally "the love of honor."

To live a quiet life would include minding "their own business." That admonition may strike us as somewhat strange, since we are constantly urged to help and care for our fellow-Christians. But the context suggests that some of the church members, having given up work, had become busybodies and were meddling in other people's affairs. Living with the hope of Christ's return should not lead to the neglect of one's earthly responsibilities. On the contrary, we must seek to fulfill our calling here on earth.

C. Working with One's Hands (vv.11b,12).

"And to work with your hands, just as we told you, so that your daily life may win the respect of outsiders and so that you will not be dependent on anybody."

If the earlier appeal was directed at the fanatics and meddlers, this one seems to be pointed at the loafers. No doubt many of the readers were artisans, engaged in some form of manual labor. Manual labor was not generally in high repute in Greek culture; it was assumed that slaves would do that. In Jewish thought work was highly regarded. Whereas it was expected that people would rise out of respect for a scholar, a craftsman engaged in his trade was exempt from getting up to show his respects, for he was doing an honorable work.

Paul may have anticipated some problems in this area and so he reminds them that they had commanded them, when they were with them, to work with their hands. If they didn't they would soon be dependent on others for their livelihood and that would give the church a bad reputation in the community. They are to live (literally "to walk") in a noble, honorable, proper way (*euschemenos*—following a good pattern). The outsiders are the non-Christians who often have a sharp eye for the faults of church members. If they are to be won for the church, believers must live in such a way that unbelievers will respect them, even when they do not yet share their faith.

Personal Response

1. *How would the desire to please God (v. 2) affect the spirit of Christian ethics?*
2. *Why are the teachings of the Scriptures necessary even when believers are anxious to please their Lord?*
3. *To the Jew Paul became a Jew and to the Greek a Greek, but in the matter of sexual relations he is uncompromising. Why?*
4. *On what grounds does Paul expect the marriage relations of Christians to be different from those of pagans (v. 4)?*
5. *Supporting others in need is an expression of Christian love. What about supporting ourselves, is that also an expression of love?*

CHAPTER SIX

THE BLESSED HOPE OF THE BELIEVER

> *Brothers, we do not want you to be ignorant about those who fall asleep, or to grieve like the rest of men, who have no hope. We believe that Jesus died and rose again and so we believe that God will bring with Jesus those who have fallen asleep in him. According to the Lord's own word, we tell you that we who are still alive, who are left till the coming of the Lord, will certainly not precede those who have fallen asleep. For the Lord himself will come down from heaven, with a loud command, with the voice of the archangel and with the trumpet call of God, and the dead in Christ will rise first. After that, we who are still alive and are left will be caught up together with them in the clouds to meet the Lord in the air. And so we will be with the Lord forever. Therefore encourage each other with these words (1 Thess. 4:13-18).*

This paragraph offers us one of the fuller descriptions of the coming of Christ at the end of the age. Even so, the passage is brief and much is left unsaid, so that we must supplement our understanding of the *parousia* from other New Testament passages.

The occasion that led Paul to give us this picture of Christ's second coming was evidently the sorrow of the Thessalonians because of the loss of loved ones. Paul expresses the hope that more light on the subject of death and the beyond will help his readers to overcome their grief.

It is hard to explain why there should have been such a gap in their knowledge about the resurrection, for certainly

Paul and his associates would not have neglected to teach so fundamental a doctrine. Could it be that the Thessalonians had understood Paul to say that the *parousia* would occur at any moment soon, and now that some of their Christian friends had died, they feared that those who were in the grave would miss this great event? Perhaps Paul's readers had received instruction on this subject but had not grasped all of its implication. In Old Testament times only those living experienced an ascension (Elijah, for example), and so the Thessalonians may have found it hard to see how people who lay buried in graves could experience the *parousia*. It may even be that some of them held that the day of the Lord had already come (cf. 2 Thess. 2:2ff.).

That the readers needed further instruction, or a clarification of earlier teachings, is clearly seen from verse 13: "Brothers, we do not want you to be ignorant about those who fall asleep." Sometimes when Paul introduces a new topic (Rom. 11:25; 1 Cor. 10:1) or when he wants to underscore some truth (Rom. 1:13; Col. 2:1; 1 Cor. 11:3), he begins by saying that he does not want his readers to be ignorant. That is, of course, an effective way of saying that he wants them to be informed.

The reason Paul wants the church to be informed on the state of those who have died is a pastoral one: so that they may not grieve like those who have no hope. Is it not true that a lot of grief is caused by ignorance, because we have not fully grasped what God's word teaches? Some of the Thessalonians grieved because they thought their loved ones were separated from them forever.

Grieving over the loss of loved ones is natural and Paul does not forbid mourning. Although Christians know that Christ has broken the power of death, funerals are not entirely joyous celebrations. However, Paul does not want us to grieve like those "who have no hope." Plato had taught the immortality of the soul and in the mystery religions there was also talk about the life to come, but the blessed hope of the gospel was not known in the Gentile world. In Ephesians 2:12 Gentiles are described as being "without hope and without God in the world." Believers, by contrast, have the blessed hope or, as Peter puts it, the living hope (1 Pet. 1:3). The word "hope" was not the most noble word in classical Greek and was sometimes understood in the sense of a wish or dream. But the Christian gospel ennobled the word and gave it content, made it concrete. In fact "hope" is so concrete that it is said to be laid up in heaven (Col. 1:5) and that we now wait for the blessed hope (Tit. 2:13).

Our passage, then, is designed to comfort the readers by informing them on the state of the dead. The dead are said to be those who have fallen asleep. "Sleep" is a euphemism for death. This figure of speech can be found in both Greek writings as well as Jewish works. When Jesus told his disciples that Lazarus was sleeping, they understood that word in the literal sense, and took that to be a sign that he was getting better. Jesus, however, had used it in the figurative sense and so he told them plainly that he had died (John 11:11). All cultures have euphemisms for death because it is such a grim reality. Since the word "sleep" is a metaphor for death we should not infer from this word that those who die in Christ are unconscious until the resurrection at the end of the age. In Philippians 1:23 Paul informs us that to die and to be with Christ is a much better state than life here on earth.

Let us now see what Paul has to say about the blessed hope of the believer. First of all he will show us that our hope is built on the death and the resurrection of Jesus Christ. Secondly, he will assure us that this hope is not illusory; it is confirmed by a word of the Lord. Then, thirdly, Paul will describe for us how this hope will be fulfilled and realized in the end. Finally, he points to the lasting comfort that finds its source in the blessed hope.

I. The Foundation of Our Hope (v. 14).

The conditional "if" should be translated as "since," for this is a true to fact condition. There is no question about our belief "that Jesus died and rose again." Christ's death and resurrection belong to the very heart of the gospel (1 Cor. 15:3-8). They are the foundation stones on which the Christian faith rests. Without the resurrection of Jesus his death would have been an unmitigated tragedy. Paul can say that we have eternal life by virtue of Christ's death (5:10), without mentioning the resurrection. However, his death would not save anyone had God not raised him from the dead, so that even when his death is mentioned alone, the resurrection must always be assumed.

Although philosophers have at times argued that there must be a life after death, such arguments are too precarious to build our hopes on. Our hopes rest on historical events: the death and resurrection of our Lord. By his resurrection he broke the power of death and thereby assures all those who are united with him in faith of eternal life with God.

Just as certain as is the death and resurrection of Jesus, argues Paul, is also the hope that "God will bring with Jesus those who sleep in him." It is possible to connect the prepositional phrase "through Jesus" with the verb "to bring," as we have it in the NIV, or to connect it with the verb "to sleep." If the latter should be correct then the meaning is that God lays his children to sleep through Jesus when they die, like a mother tucking in her child for the night.

But we are also not certain about the meaning of the verb "to bring." Does he mean that God will bring back from heaven those who have died in the faith and who are now with Christ? The meaning may also be that he will bring them from the grave when Christ returns in glory. Another possibility is that God brings the believer who dies together with Jesus at the moment of death. In that event this is a reference to the intermediate state of the saints between their death and their resurrection. Of one thing, however, we can be sure: God will not abandon his children when they die. The death and resurrection of Jesus gives us solid grounds for holding that our hope of eternal life with God will not prove to be an illusion.

II. The Certitude of Our Hope (v. 15).

"According to the Lord's own word, we tell you that we who are still alive, who are left till the coming of the Lord, will certainly not precede those who have fallen asleep."

Just what is meant by a "word of the Lord," is not certain. Did Paul have a direct revelation from the Lord? Or, is the apostle referring to some unwritten word of Jesus? That some sayings of Jesus were remembered even though they had not been recorded in the Gospels can be seen, for example, from Acts 20:35. It could be, too, that Paul is taking an Old Testament word of God spoken by some prophet about the day of the Lord and applying it here in a new way. He could be quoting a Christian prophet, too, or some apocalyptic work. There is nothing in our Gospels that resembles this word of the Lord, although Jesus did speak clearly about his coming in glory as well as of the resurrection of the dead. Whatever the background, Paul is conscious of the fact that he is speaking the Lord's mind, and that gives the blessed hope great certitude.

What then is the word of the Lord? "We who are still alive" when Jesus comes will not have any advantage over those who have died in the faith. Critics have accused Paul of error since he seems to think he will still be alive when Christ returns, for he includes himself in the "we." But in 5:10 he mentions death as an alternate possibility, "whether we are awake or asleep," i.e. whether we live or die. Rather than accusing Paul of error, we should make his language our own. On the one hand, we always live with the hope that he will come when we are still alive; on the other hand, we are realistic enough to know that should the Lord tarry, we will die some day.

And should we die we will not be at a disadvantage when the Lord comes. That must have been the concern Paul's readers had. Some of their loved ones had died and they feared they had thereby lost out on something very important. Paul says, No! Never! (He uses a double negative to make his denial even stronger.) "We shall not all sleep," he writes to the Corinthians (1 Cor. 15:51), i.e. we will not all die; some will be alive when Christ returns. But, Paul adds, "we shall all be changed." At the *parousia* both the dead and the living saints will receive new and glorified bodies, since flesh and blood cannot enter the eternal kingdom (1 Cor. 15:50). This assurance that there is life beyond the grave gives meaning and purpose to our lives here on earth.

III. The Fulfilment of our Hope (vv. 16,17).

In verses 16 and 17 Paul defines for his readers what the Christian can look forward to and so we speak of it as the fulfillment of the living hope. Basically there are three great events that the church looks forward to: 1. The coming of Christ; 2. The resurrection of the saints; 3. The rapture of the church.

A. The Coming of Christ (v. 16a).

"For the Lord himself will come down from heaven, with a loud command, with the voice of the archangel and with the trumpet call of God."

The *parousia* of our Lord is described largely in pictures drawn from the Old Testament and Jewish apocalyptic. It is important to note that the Lord himself will usher in the consummation of this age, and not a human being or human power. Caesar also was called "lord" and he made royal visits (*parousiai*) to cities in the empire, accompanied by the fanfare of trumpets. It may be that this background played into the choice of Paul's words as he describes the coming of Christ at the end of the age.

That Christ will descend from heaven has already been stated in 1:10, and that is still appropriate terminology for someone standing on this earth. Today Christ is exalted, seated at the right hand of God. On the last day he will come "with a shouted command." This is a military metaphor, an officer's order. The word rings with excitement, urgency and authority. The word *keleusma* (summons, shouted command) is not found anywhere else in the New Testament. Paul does not say who gives the command, whether God or Christ, but when this command is given the heavenly armies are set in motion. We are reminded of Revelation 19 where Christ appears on a white horse followed by the armies of heaven.

Another attendant circumstance of the *parousia* is "the voice of an archangel." We do not know which archangel. Michael is the only archangel mentioned by name in the New Testament (Jude 9). Perhaps the meaning is that the command is given as if it were given by an archangel, i.e. with authority and finality. Angels are the celestial attendants upon the great historical events of redemption history— Christ's birth, his temptation, his suffering in Gethsemane, the resurrection, the ascension, and finally, the *parousia*.

It may be that the voice of the archangel is addressed to the dead. Jesus said that on that last day "the dead would hear the voice of the Son of God and those who hear will live" (John 5:25).

Also, Christ returns when the "trumpet of God" sounds. The trumpet plays an important role in the Old Testament. The trumpet was blown when the people of God assembled (Ex. 19:16,17). The great sabbatical month was introduced with the blowing of trumpets. It comes to be associated especially with the day of the Lord (Joel 2:1). The day of the Lord is described as a day of trumpet blasts (Zeph. 1:16). And so it is associated with the *parousia* in the New Testament. Jesus said that when the Son of Man would come in glory he would "send his angels with a loud trumpet and they will gather his elect from the four winds, from one end of the heavens to the other" (Matt. 24:31).

B. The Resurrection of the Saints (v. 16b).

"And the dead in Christ will rise first."

It should be noted that Paul thinks of the dead as being "in Christ." Not even death can separate them from Christ. They were "in Christ" here on earth and they remain "in Christ" even in death.

Clearly Paul deals only with the dead in Christ in this passage; that he holds also to the resurrection of all people can be seen from other passages. In Revelation 20, John distinguishes between the first resurrection and the resurrection after the millennium. Those who take part in the first resurrection, the believers, have escaped the power of "the second death," i.e. eternal death. Paul leaves all that out, since he is not writing a complete biblical theology, but is addressing the problems of the Thessalonians. Also, Paul says nothing about the resurrection body; for information on that subject one must read 1 Corinthians 15.

C. The Rapture of the Church (v. 17).

"After that, we who are still alive and are left will be caught up together with them in the clouds to meet the Lord in the air. And so we will be with the Lord forever."

The noun "rapture" is not found in the Bible, but we have a verb (*harpazo*) which means to take and carry off, to snatch away. Under the influence of the verb *rapio*, which is found in the Latin Vulgate, the word "rapture" has entered our theological vocabulary (and in this sense it does not mean happiness and excitement). That the bodies of the living saints who will be taken up when Christ returns will also be changed is left unsaid here (cf. 1 Cor. 15:51).

The living saints together with the resurrected believers will be caught in the clouds. "Clouds" are a familiar figure of speech in the Bible for the presence of God. When God appeared to Israel he appeared in a thick cloud. The cloud conveys both hiddenness and majesty. Moreover, the cloud became connected with the day of the Lord. The day of the Lord is a day of clouds (Ez. 30:3). The Son of Man comes in clouds of glory (Dan. 7:13; Mark 13:26; 14:62). "Behold, he comes with the clouds," says John (Rev. 1:7).

When God appeared on Mt. Sinai he came in a thick cloud; the trumpets sounded and the people of God gathered for a meeting with God. At that time only Moses and the elders ascended the mountain. Here all of God's people ascend for a meeting with the Lord in the air. The word for "meeting" (*apantesis*) is carefully chosen. When a *parousia* of Caesar took place there was usually a reception, a meeting, outside the city. City officials would go out to meet him and accompany Caesar and his entourage into the city with great pomp and circumstance. The word is used in a non-technical sense in Acts 28:15, and once more in an eschatological setting. In the Parable of the Ten Maidens we hear them say, "Here's the bridegroom! Come out to meet him" (Matt. 25:6).

The meeting with the Lord takes place "in the air." The word "air" is probably used in a metaphorical sense like the word "clouds." In any case this is not the language of astrophysics but of theology. It may in fact be that Paul thought of "air" as the abode of evil spirits and the realm of Satan (Eph. 2:2). If so, Paul may be saying that on the very terrain where evil powers have held sway so long, the church will celebrate its final triumph.

However we may understand the details of the *parousia* of our Lord, his coming fulfills the highest hopes of the saints through all ages: to be "together with the Lord for ever" (v. 17b). While we are in our present bodies, says Paul, we are away from the Lord (2 Cor. 5:6), but when the last day comes we will be at home with the Lord (2 Cor. 5:8). Although we have fellowship with Christ even while we are in our present mortal state, it is only a foretaste of what we shall experience when we see him "face to face" (1 Cor. 13:12).

IV. The Comfort of Our Hope (v. 18).

"Therefore encourage each other with these words."
The word *parakaleo* can mean to encourage but also to comfort. Here we can see clearly the pastoral purpose of this letter. Eschatological teachings in the New Testament are always given with a practical intent and not to satisfy our curiosity or to encourage speculation about details that have not been disclosed.

Death is an awful enemy that makes an end of all that is precious to us here in our earthly life. Although Christ broke the power of death by his resurrection, death is the last enemy to be put out of commission (1 Cor. 15:26). And so as we face the death of loved ones and also our own death, we take comfort from "these words." We have a papyrus letter in which Irene writes to Tannophris to comfort him at the loss of a loved one. It ends with these words: "But nevertheless against such things one can do nothing. Therefore, comfort one another." How sad! What is missing is "these words." The gospel brings us hope because we have "these words," which are trustworthy; we can stake our lives on them. When Christ comes our deepest longings will be satisfied and our highest hopes fulfilled.

Personal Response

1. *Is it proper for believers to grieve when loved ones die?*
2. *How can fuller knowledge about the state of the dead ameliorate our sorrows (cf. v. 13)?*
3. *How does the resurrection of Christ guarantee the resurrection of all people?*
4. *Should we expect the Lord to come in our life-time (cf. v.15)?*
5. *"We shall be forever with the Lord." What dimension does that promise add to the hope of new heaven and earth, the new Jerusalem, and other aspects mentioned by John in the Revelation?*

CHAPTER SEVEN

CHRIST'S COMING AT THE END OF THE AGE

> *Now, brothers, about times and dates we do not need to write to you, for you know very well that the day of the Lord will come like a thief in the night. While people are saying, 'Peace and safety, destruction will come on them suddenly, as labor pains on a pregnant woman, and they will not escape.*
>
> *But you, brothers, are not in darkenss so that this day should surprise you like a thief. You are all sons of the light and sons of the day. We do not belong to the night or to the darkness. So then, let us not be like others, who are asleep, but let us be alert and self-controlled. For those who sleep, sleep at night, and those who get drunk, get drunk at night. But since we belong to the day, let us be self-controlled, putting on faith and love as a breastplate, and the hope of salvation as a helmet. For God did not appoint us to suffer wrath but to receive salvation through our Lord Jesus Christ. He died for us so that, whether we are awake or asleep, we may live together with him. Therefore, encourage one another and build each other up, just as in fact you are doing (1 Thess. 5:1-11).*

Although the word *parousia* does not occur in the passage we are about to study, Paul continues the theme of Christ's coming at the end of the age. In chapter 4 Paul addresses the question of the state of the dead in Christ; in 5:1-11 he speaks to the question of preparedness, readiness for the last day. Watchfulness is seen not in excitement and alarm, but rather in spiritual alertness.

Whether the Thessalonians had speculated about the time of the Lord's coming is not known, but from the way Paul addresses the question of setting dates for the *parousia* it is not impossible. The apostle makes it very clear that date-setting is not something Christians should engage in. Jesus, in his Olivet Discourse, had made it very plain that "no one knows about that day or hour" (Mark 13:32), and for that reason his followers should always be on guard and alert. Paul begins this passage on Christ's coming at the end of the age with some comments on the indefiniteness of the hour.

I. The Indefiniteness of the Time of Christ's Coming (vv. 1-3).

  A. Knowing the Time (vv. 1,2).

"Now, brothers, about times and dates we do not need to write to you."

Paul uses two words for "time" in his opening statement. Originally *chronos* meant time in its durative or quantitative aspect, and *kairos* in its qualitative aspect, critical time, opportune time. Whether that distinction is to be made here is not certain for the phrase seems to have been familiar. Jesus told his disciples, when they asked for the time when eschatological events would unfold, that it was not for them "to know times and seasons" (Acts 1:7). The Old Testament, in the Greek translation, also has this phrase (Dan. 2:21; 7:25).

Why does Paul feel no need to write to the Thessalonians about times and seasons? Because they "knew very well that the day of the Lord will come like a thief in the night." Evidently Paul had told them that the Lord would come unannounced. They knew this *akribos* (an adverb that means they knew it precisely, exactly, accurately). Not that they knew exactly when this age would end, but they knew that the day of the Lord would occur unannounced.

The day of the Lord is a common expression in the Old Testament and is used here as a synonym for the *parousia*. Sometimes the abbreviated form "the day" is used (cf. v. 4). These are but a few of the many words used to signify the end of the age. In fact it is also called simply "the end" (1 Cor. 15:24). In the Old Testament the day of the Lord has two aspects: it is a day of judgment for the ungodly, and a day of salvation for the true people of God. These two dimensions are found in the New Testament as well; in fact, our passage has both (cf. v. 3, 9). Israel had the notion that the day of the Lord would be a glorious day, whereas the Gentiles would suffer God's wrath. Amos had to correct that view (5:18-20), for God, he explains, would not draw the line between Jew and Gentile, but between the godly and the ungodly.

The day of the Lord is not a "human day" (1 Cor. 4:3). In fact on that great day of the Lord humans will have nothing to say. Today individuals and nations may rebel against God, but when the day of the Lord comes they will have to bow humbly before the Judge of all the earth.

And this great day is "coming." It's already on its way. It's always near. It comes like a thief in the night. There may be a touch of irony in that. It may be that Paul is saying, you know the time of Christ's coming as accurately as you know when a thief will strike. To come as a thief does not mean that Christ has a sinister purpose in mind, as does a thief. It is simply a figure of speech to underscore the fact that Christ's coming will be unannounced. Paul is not the only one who makes use of that simile. Jesus uses it (Matt. 24:43), as does Peter (2 Pet. 3:10) and John (Rev. 3:3; 16:15).

The simile of the thief in the night does not mean that the *parousia* will take place at night, as some people thought in the early centuries of the Christian church, before it was known that we lived on a planet on which it is always day in half the world. The word "night" has been understood by some readers to refer to the moral darkness that is expected to spread over this world before Christ's appearance at the end of the age. There is an element of truth in that, for Paul expects the Man of Lawless to make his appearance in the end, but the word "night" in verse 2 is simply part of the figurative language. Christians are tempted from time to time to speculate about the closeness of the end, when they face a tide of evil in their society. But we cannot establish the date of Christ's coming on the basis of how much evil we see around us.

B. Disregarding the Time (v. 3).

"While people are saying, 'Peace and safety,' destruction will come upon them suddenly, as labor pains on a pregnant woman, and they will not escape."

Paul does not spell out who will say, "Peace and security," but obviously not believers. The language is reminiscent of the false prophets of the Old Testament and their false cry of peace (Jer. 6:14; 8:11; Ez. 13:10; Mic. 3:5). It may in fact be a proverbial saying. "Peace" is used here in its secular sense as a synonym of security.

This may be Paul's way of saying what Jesus had said about the last days: "As it was in the days of Noah, so will it be in the days of the Son of man. They ate, they drank, they married, they were given in marriage, until the day when Noah entered the ark and the flood came and destroyed them all" (Luke 17:26). These were otherwise legitimate activities, but when people are completely earth-bound and are devoid of all spiritual interests, they look for security in the things of this world.

Destruction will suddenly come upon the ungodly, who have paid no attention to the gospel. Sudden destruction is the equivalent of eternal destruction in 2 Thess. 1:9. The suddenness is illustrated by the simile of a pregnant women who is suddenly caught in the pangs of childbirth. The "thief in the night" comes unexpected; the pangs of childbirth are not unexpected, even though they come on suddenly. The emphasis lies rather on the inevitability of birth, once the labor pangs set in. "They shall not escape," meaning, that when the day of the Lord comes it will be too late to repent; judgment is inescapable for those who were indifferent to the gospel.

II. The Confident Expectation of Christ's Coming (vv. 4-8).

In contrast to the ungodly for whom the day of the Lord is no pleasant prospect, stand the children of light, the believers, who need not fear this day.

A. The Preparation (vv. 4,5).

"But you, brothers, are not in darkness so that this day should surprise you like a thief. You are all sons of the light and sons of the day. We do not belong to the night or to the darkness."

Although Christ will come as a thief in the night he will not catch us by surprise. Not that we know when he will come, but because we are not in darkness, the day will not catch us unawares. "Darkness" stands for evil, "light" for holiness. Sometimes darkness also means ignorance and light means knowledge. Here, however, it looks as if Paul is comparing the ungodly (v. 3) with the godly (vv.4,5).

"We are all sons of the light and sons of day." The "we" includes all believers. To be a son of something is a Semitic way of saying that we are characterized, in this case, by light and day. Whether we are prepared for Christ's coming depends then on whether we belong to the darkness, the realm of evil, or to the light, the kingdom of God. But, as so often in the writings of Paul, the imperative is based on an indicative. We are to become what we in fact are already. Since we are children of light, we need to live like people of the day.

B. The Exhortation (vv. 6-8).

"So then, let us not be like others, who are asleep, but let us be alert and self-controlled" (v. 6).

As in 4:13 he designates the ungodly as "rest." The rest, he says, are spiritually asleep. To be asleep means that they are unconscious of the great event at the end of the age or indifferent to it. It is the sleep of false security, moral and spiritual turpitude.

Believers, who have come out of the kingdom of darkness into the kingdom of light, must, by contrast, watch and be alert. Three times in verses 6-8 Paul uses the hortatory subjunctive and so includes himself in the exhortation: "Let us." To watch does not mean that we feverishly occupy our minds constantly with the Lord's return, but it means to remain spiritually awake. We don't have to "wallow" in end-times events to remain spiritually alert.

"For those who sleep, sleep at night, and those who get drunk, get drunk at night." This is a factual observation of what happens in ordinary life: people sleep at night and some get drunk at night. Such persons are oblivious to what is going on. Christians, who belong to the day must live lives that are in keeping with their standing, as children of the light. Drunkenness suggests immoderate and immoral behavior; sleep suggests spiritual dullness. Neither is commensurate with the believer's calling.

"But since we belong to the day, let us be self-controlled" (v. 8a). The exhortation to sobriety, spiritual alertness, is repeated here from verse 6, for it leads naturally to the next metaphor, that of a soldier standing guard. Vigilance evidently suggested the Roman sentry to Paul, and so we have the exhortation to be properly armed. "Putting on faith and love as a breastplate, and the hope of salvation as a helmet" (v. 8b).

The Christian life is often pictured as a warfare, because the kingdom of darkness continues to wield power, even though the outcome of the battle was secured at the cross and the resurrection. Whether the language in our text was taken from observing Roman soldiers or whether it was taken from the Old Testament, where God is sometimes portrayed as warrior (cf. Isa. 59:17), is not certain. The armor we are to put on is faith, love and hope, the three Christian graces which we have encountered earlier in this letter (cf. 1:3)."The breastplate of faith and love" means that faith and love function as the breastplate and "the hope of salvation" suggests that salvation is the object of our hope (objective genitive). It is quite appropriate to confess that we have already been saved but there is yet a salvation ready to be revealed in the last time (1 Pet. 1:5), and for that we hope.

With this kind of spiritual armor we can look confidently forward to Christ's coming at the end of the age. If we have become children of the day and walk like children of light, we need not fear the *parousia*; for when Christ comes he will deliver us from wrath (1:10).

III. The Theological Foundations of Christ's Coming (vv. 9,10.

Paul now gives us some of the theological underpinnings for our hope of the return of Christ at the end of the age. Lest any of his readers should feel uneasy at the thought of the day of the Lord, Paul assures them, first, that God did not appoint them to wrath but to receive salvation. Second, Christ died for us to secure our salvation. On that basis the believers can rejoice at the thought that some day they will enter the eternal kingdom.

A. God's Salvatory Plan (v. 9).

"For God did not appoint us to suffer wrath but to receive salvation through our Lord Jesus Christ."

Early on in this letter (1:4) Paul spoke of the election of the Thessalonians; here he says that we are "destined" not to wrath but to salvation. It is a way of underscoring that salvation is entirely by divine grace. God did not choose us to condemn us, but to save us.

The day of the Lord is often seen as a day of wrath when God will judge the ungodly. Believers, however, have been destined to "acquire" salvation. Again this does not mean that salvation is not a present possession, but here salvation is seen in its future dimension. This salvation can be obtained only through our Lord Jesus Christ, not by our own efforts. And to underscore that truth, Paul recalls the great historical event: the death of Christ.

B. Christ's Substitutionary Death (v. 10).

"He died for us so that, whether we are awake or asleep, we may live together with him."

This is the only place in the Thessalonian letters where the atoning death of Christ is mentioned (that he died is mentioned in 4:14, but not that he died "for us"). The almost casual way in which Paul brings in the substitutionary death of Christ suggests that it lay at the heart of his message and that the readers were well acquainted with this fundamental truth.

It has been suggested that in these early letters Paul had not yet developed his theology of the cross as this is found in some of his later correspondence. However, the cross was so central in his proclamation that even in the midst of an eschatological passage he touches upon this pivotal point in redemption history. What makes Christ's death so significant is the fact that he did not die for any crimes that he had committed but he died "for us." His was a substitutionary death. Without his death we too would be exposed to the wrath of God, but by dying for us he took our place and now delivers us from wrath (1:10).

The purpose of his death is that we should "live with him." To live means more than simply to exist; it refers to a new quality of life—eternal life. He died so that we might live. Although Paul does not mention the resurrection, that is assumed, for without the resurrection Christ's death would be untold tragedy. Moreover, we would not be able to live with him had he not broken the power of death by rising from the grave. To live with him is another way of saying "we shall be forever with the Lord" (4:17).

This glorious prospect is ours regardless of whether "we are awake or asleep." In verse 6 Paul used these metaphors to speak of spiritual and moral alertness. In verse 7 sleep refers to physical sleep in contrast to being physically awake. But here in verse 10 these words are used in a third way: waking and sleeping mean being alive or being dead. Since those who are alive at Christ's coming will have no advantage over the dead in Christ, it doesn't really matter whether we die before Christ returns or whether we are alive when he comes. Either way we will live with him forever.

God wills our salvation (v. 9), and through the death of his Son he made salvation possible. Those are solid bases for our hope.

IV. The Practical Implications of Christ's Coming (v. 11).

"Therefore encourage one another and build each other up, just as in fact you are doing."

The conclusion to this paragraph on watchfulness is very similar to the one at the end of Paul's description of the *parousia* (4:18). There the word *parakaleo* seems to have the meaning of comfort and consolation, for the passage was addressed to those who evidently were grieving because of the death of loved ones. Here, however, the word seems to have the meaning of exhortation and encouragement.

How they are to exhort or encourage one another is not stated, but we should note that it is reciprocal ("one another"). This is not only the duty of the leaders and teachers of the church but every member has a responsibility to encourage his or her fellow-members. It is by encouraging our fellow Christians to walk the Christian way and to carry out their mission in the world that we build each other up, edify each other.

As so often when Paul gives a word of admonition, he adds a word of commendation. Here, too, Paul recognizes that they are in fact doing what he is asking them to do. However, there is always room for growth.

Personal Response

1. How do we respond to those who are constantly setting dates for the Lord's return?
2. How do we keep our hope of Christ's return alive?
3. How do we properly "wait" for the Lord's coming?
4. Why do we not have to fear the day of the Lord?
5. How can we encourage one another and build each other up?

CHAPTER EIGHT

THE SPIRITUAL LIFE OF THE CHURCH

> *Now we ask you, brothers, to respect those who work hard among you, who are over you in the Lord and who admonish you. Hold them in the highest regard in love because of their work. Live in peace with each other. And we urge you, brothers, warn those who are idle, encourage the timid, help the weak, be patient with everyone. Make sure that nobody pays back wrong for wrong, but always try to be kind to each other and to everyone else.*
>
> *Be joyful always; pray continually; give thanks in all circumstances, for this is God's will for you in Christ Jesus. Do not put out the Spirit's fire; do not treat prophecies with contempt. Test everything. Hold on to the good. Avoid every kind of evil.*
>
> *May God himself, the God of peace, sanctify you through and through. May your whole spirit, soul and body be kept blameless at the coming of our Lord Jesus Christ. The one who calls you is faithful and he will do it.*
>
> *Brothers, pray for us. Greet all the brothers with a holy kiss. I charge you before the Lord to have this letter read to all the brothers.*
>
> *The grace of our Lord Jesus Christ be with you (1 Thess. 5:12-28).*

The hope of Christ's return at the end of the age should not make believers into visionaries who have lost all interest in the life of the church here on earth and who wait only for the end to come. The blessed hope moves us to fulfill our calling here on earth; it sustains us in our trials; it gives meaning and purpose to even the mundane activities of the work-a-day world.

In this closing paragraph Paul brings his readers down to earth and shows them ways in which they can build each other up— the closing admonition of the previous passage (5:11). His admonitions give us glimpses into the inner life of the church in the first century. He begins with a word on the ministry of church leaders (vv. 12,13). He then outlines some of the ways in which the members of the church are to express their responsibilities toward one another (vv. 14,15). Also, he gives us an insight into the worship services of the early church (vv. 16-22), and offers a prayer for the Thessalonians (vv. 23,24). The letter closes with a few words of instruction and the final greeting (vv. 25-28).

I. The Ministry of the Leaders (vv. 12,13).

A. Respect for the Leaders (v. 12).

"Now we ask you, brothers, to respect those who work hard among you, who are over you in the Lord and who admonish you" (v. 12).

The word "brothers" (which includes the sisters) occurs five times in our passage (vv. 12,14,25,26,27) and reminds us strongly of the fact that the church is a family in which members have mutual responsibilities.

For a church to function harmoniously there must be leadership, and the leaders must be respected if the church is to grow. And so the Thessalonians are asked to "know" their leaders. To know their leaders does not mean simply to "get to know" them but means to "acknowledge" them as leaders. When a congregation chooses a leader it must demonstrate an appropriate attitude toward such a person.

There is a great variety of names used for leaders of the church in the New Testament. They are called "bishops" (Phil. 1:1; 1 Tim. 3:1), or "elders" (Tit. 1:5), or "pastors"

(Eph. 4:11). In our passage Paul is not concerned about what they are called, but rather about what they do. Their work is described by three participles: laboring, leading/caring, and admonishing. We have already had the noun "labor" (1:3; 2:9) to describe both the church's and the apostle's efforts to build the church; now we get the verb *kopiao* (in the active it means "to labor" and in the passive "to tire"). According to 1 Timothy 5:17 elders who labor in teaching are to be given double honor.

Another aspect of their ministry is "to be over you in the Lord." The verb literally means "to stand before," and then "to preside." However, the word also has the meaning of "caring." In 1 Timothy 3:5 "managing" one's household is in parallel construction with "caring" for the church of God. Leaders do their work "in the Lord." They serve in his name and in the strength that he supplies. Also, they serve in the spirit of Jesus who came not to be served but to serve and to give his life a ransom for many (Mark 10:45).

The third participle (*noutheteo*) means, literally, "to put into mind." It includes admonition, instruction, rebuke, discipline, comfort and encouragement. It's a word that speaks of encouragement to good behavior and of warning against bad behavior. Although there may be the sound of harshness in it, that does not have to be the case at all. Paul uses this word to cover the many aspects of his three-year ministry in Ephesus (Acts 20:31).

Whether Paul had assisted the Thessalonians in choosing their leaders when he was still with them is not known. Obviously they were chosen from the ranks of the congregation. Although Paul later warns against choosing novices (1 Tim. 3:6), to begin with, leaders would be relatively young Christians who had the gift of leadership. One might infer from the admonition to acknowledge their leaders that there was a problem along this line in the Thessalonian church. Again, such exhortations may have been given simply to prevent chaos in the church.

B. Esteem for Their Ministry (vv. 13).

"Hold them in the highest regard in love because of their work."

To esteem them "in love," is quite different from respecting someone out of fear. Moreover, it is "on account of their work" that they are to be honored. It is not because of their social standing, their birth, or even their gifts that they are necessarily to be esteemed, but because of the work they do in the body of Christ.

Esteem must, of course, be earned, and Paul assumes that the leaders do their tasks faithfully. He says nothing here about what the church should do when leaders fail to do their tasks. Even when God's servants do their work in weakness, they deserve the respect of the congregation, because they exercise pastoral care for the sake of the members.

And if leaders are to do their work with joy then the members must "live in peace with each other." A manuscript variant reading changes the admonition to "live in peace with them," but it does not have strong support.

II. The Responsibility of the Members (vv. 14,15).

These two verses begin very much like verses 12 and 13, although the verb "ask" (v. 12) now becomes "exhort" (v. 14). The admonition here is also directed at the entire congregation ("brothers"), and that suggests that Paul does not expect the leaders to do all the work with the congregation reduced to observer status. There are some aspects of pastoral care that are the responsibility of all the members of the congregation. What are the kind of things that comprise the ministry of the laity?

A. Admonition.

"We urge you, brothers, warn those who are idle."
The word for warn (*noutheteo*) is the same word that was used to describe the task of the leaders. Perhaps "warn" is too strong a word. It could also mean to advise, to instruct, to admonish. The word for "idlers" (*ataktos*) means simply to be "out of step," and could be translated as careless or disorderly. It so happens, however, that in the papyri the word is used also for the shirkers, the idlers, and that is how the NIV renders it. In 2 Thess. 3:7 and 11 it clearly means idlers; here it could mean either. In fact, it could have a double meaning, for idleness often leads to disorderly behavior.

B. Encouragement.

"Encourage the timid." Who were the timid? (*Oligopsuchos* means "little souls".) They must have been those who were weighed down by fear, worry or discouragement. Perhaps they found persecution for their faith too much for themselves, or they were grieving over the deaths of loved ones. There are wounded hearts in every congregation, and so the ministry of encouragement is of vital significance.

C. Assistance.

"Help the weak." The verb means to be attached to, to be faithful, to stand by, ever ready to help. Although the word "weak" can also mean "sick," we should not limit the word to that meaning. Perhaps the whole range of physical, emotional and spiritual weaknesses are included. There are those who are subject to special temptations; there are the overly scrupulous who often do not know what to do; there are the poor who are economically weak. "We who are strong," writes Paul to the Romans, "should bear the infirmities of the weak" (Rom. 15:1).

D. Patience.

"Be patient with everyone." *Makrothumeo* means to be long-suffering, long-tempered, patient. Patience is a fruit of the Spirit (Gal. 5:22). It is an expression of love (1 Cor. 13:4). God is long-suffering and we must imitate him (Rom. 2:4). Whether the word "all" should be restricted to the various groups he has just mentioned who need our help, or whether he has all members of the church in mind, or perhaps even all human beings, is not made clear, but the word must not be limited to those people needing help. The theme of long-suffering is expanded in the next admonition.

E. Forgiveness.

"Make sure that nobody pays back wrong for wrong." From the days of Lamech (Gen. 4:24), who sang of revenge in his sword song, revenge has characterized human society. Jesus clearly taught that this was wrong (Matt. 5:39,44) and the apostles upheld this teaching (cf. Rom. 12:17-21). The antidote to revenge and retaliation for personal wrongs is forgiveness. Jesus forgave those who put him to death, as did Stephen, and a host of others who suffered innocently and did not retaliate but, like Jesus, entrusted themselves to him who judges justly (1 Pet. 2:23).

F. Goodness.

"Always try to be kind to each other and to everyone else." Literally the text reads: "Always pursue the good." The imperative "pursue" is in the present tense, suggesting that this is to be not an occasional act but a way of life. Perhaps the command is not too different from "pursue love" (1 Cor. 14:1). Love does no wrong to the neighbor (Rom. 13:10). "To each other" would refer to the members of the church; "to everyone" goes beyond that, to embrace also the outside community. A church in which the members assume responsibility for the life and welfare of their fellow-members will certainly make a deep impression on the community in which it lives and people will feel attracted to the church.

III. The Worship of the Congregation (vv. 16-22).

What Paul has said thus far about the life of the church applies to its day-by-day existence, when the church is scattered. He will now address some aspects of the church's life when it is gathered. Some of the exhortations that now follow could, of course, be applied individually just as well as corporately. The exhortations to have this letter read in the church (v. 27), as well as the greeting with the holy kiss (v. 26) also apply to the gathered congregation, but we will mention them in the conclusion.

A. Joy (v. 16).

"Be joyful always."
After four imperatives in verse 14 we now have three more in close succession. The first is to rejoice at all times. As we saw in 1:6, Christian joy is possible even in the midst of pain. We are "as sorrowing yet as always rejoicing" (2 Cor. 6:10). Joy is a fruit of the Spirit. It is not to be equated with happiness or laughter. It comes from deeper springs, from the Holy Spirit. In our passage we may have a call to come before God's presence with joy (Ps. 95:1). Christian joy is sustained by the assurance of ultimate salvation, the hope of the eternal kingdom.

B. Prayer (v. 17).

"Pray continually."
In a formal sense this is quite impossible, for the believer has other responsibilities besides praying. But we

should always feel the need of turning to God. Paul himself worked day and night (2:9), yet he lived his entire life in dependence on God. Besides uttered prayers there is the groaning of the Spirit within us (Rom. 8:26). The believer is well advised to have stated times of prayer, but when we live our lives in dependence on God there will be silent or ejaculatory prayers even in the course of our daily duties. Here in our passage Paul may in fact have corporate praying in mind, where the congregation or groups within the church join together to pray for the needs of the church and the world.

C. Thanksgiving (v. 18).

"Give thanks in all circumstances, for this is God's will for you in Christ Jesus."

Thanksgiving should be an integral part of praying. The church, of course, may have special times of thanksgiving, as does the Christian family or the individual. In fact the Lord's Supper came to be called the Eucharist (which is the word used here for thanksgiving—*eucharisteo*), although that is not likely to be the meaning in our text.

To be thankful at all times or in all circumstances obviously does not mean that we thank God for evil, for accidents, for tragedies. However, even in the midst of evil and tragedy we can be thankful, for we know that we are in the hands of a heavenly Father who has promised to work for the good of his children in all circumstances (Rom. 8:28).

"This is God's will for you in Christ Jesus" should be applied to all three imperatives (rejoice, pray and give thanks) and not restricted to thanksgiving alone.

D. Prophecy (vv. 19-22).

There follow now another five imperatives and they all appear to be interrelated. The first is in the form of a prohibition: "Do not put out the Spirit's fire." Since prophecy is mentioned right after this prohibition, we should probably think of the manfestation of the Spirit in its gifts. To despise prophecy would be one way of quenching the Spirit. Could it be that some of the Thessalonians were revelling in the gifts of the Spirit and that others, out of reaction to these excesses, were putting the Spirit's fire out?

In any case, prophecy is not to be despised (v. 20). Prophecy covers a wide range of meanings, but here it seems to refer to the proclamation of the will of God in the congregation. Prophecy is a gift of the Spirit given for the edification of the church. It may in fact also be the means by which the unbeliever is reached with the gospel (1 Cor. 14:24). Old Testament prophets and the apostles spoke with divine authority. They have left us a rich legacy in the written Scriptures. Today those who have the prophetic gift should strive to interpret and to apply the truths of the Scriptures. We do not have people who receive direct revelation from God as did "the apostles and prophets" (Eph. 2:20) upon whom the church is built.

The kind of prophecy Paul speaks of in our text is not the primary but the secondary kind and must not be simply equated with the word of God, for then there would be no need for the church to examine what was being said. Paul's counsel to the Corinthians is: "Let two or three prophets speak; the others should weigh carefully what is said" (1 Cor. 14:29). Here, too, we have the exhortation "to test everything." The congregation is to evaluate what is being said in the name of the Spirit. There are, of course, believers who have a special gift of discernment, but here the entire congregation is addressed.

Once the hearers have examined what the prophet said, to see whether it agrees with Scripture, they are urged to "hold on to the good."

There is a so-called unwritten saying of Jesus that was well-known among some of the early Church Fathers that goes as follows: "Be good money-changers; keep the good metal, and refuse the spurious coin." That kind of saying may lie in the background here, for after urging the readers to cling to that which is good, he advises them to "hold back" from evil in every form. Although the exhortation to refrain from evil of any kind may be applied quite broadly, here it seems to refer to the words of the Christian prophets. After examining them, the good is to be held fast, but the evil in every form is to be avoided.

IV. The Prayer of the Apostle (vv. 23,24).

Paul begins the conclusion of his letter with a wish-prayer. "May God himself, the God of peace, sanctify you through and through. May your whole spirit, soul and body be kept blameless at the coming of our Lord Jesus Christ" (v. 23). Repeatedly Paul calls God "the God of peace" (Rom. 15:33; 16:20; 2 Cor. 13:11; Phil. 4:9). Behind the Greek word "peace" lies the Hebrew *shalom,* and so to pray to the God of peace is to appeal to the source of all well-being for his children.

The apostle prays for the complete sanctification of his readers. Also, he prays that they may be kept so that they may be blameless on the day when Christ returns. These two petitions are but two aspects of the same concern. Paul had already prayed for their sanctification earlier in the letter (3:13). Also, he had explained that santification was God's will for them (4:3). Here he prays that God might complete the work that he had begun in their lives and sanctify them "completely."

Paul expands on this emphasis of complete sanctification by mentioning "the spirit and the soul and the body." One need not infer from these three anthropological terms that Paul held to a trichotomous view of man. It is designed, rather, to stress the totality of the human being. (Compare the four aspects of the human personality in Mark 12:30.) In 3:13 he prays that their "hearts" might be santified; here we have spirit, soul and body. He asks that their entire personality be preserved blameless for the *parousia* of our Lord. The passive voice of the verb to "keep" suggests that it is by the power of God that the believers are preserved in holiness for the day of Jesus Christ.

Should any of the readers wonder how Paul could pray with such confidence, his bold confession in verse 25 explains that: "The one who calls you is faithful and he will do it." God calls us not only from darkness to light at the beginning of the Christian life, but he keeps on calling us throughout our life here on earth; indeed, he calls us into his kingdom and his glory (2:12). What God begins he completes; he is faithful.

CONCLUSION

1. The Request (v. 25).

"Brothers, pray for us."

After praying for them several times, even while writing his letter, he now asks his converts to pray for him. Between Paul and the churches he established there was a mutual bond of intercession. In spite of his high calling as apostle, his giftedness, his maturity, he still feels the need for the prayers of his friends. A very human touch!

2. The Greeting (v. 26).

"Greet all the brothers with a holy kiss." "Brothers" is used here (as in v. 25) in its inclusive sense, meaning also "sisters." The kiss as a form of greeting was common in Paul's day. Greetings take on many different cultural forms. The adjective "holy" adds a religious dimension to the greeting of Christians. Since members of the church belong to the family of God they greet each other not only as human beings but as "Christians." They stand closely related to one another in Christ and so they greet each other warmly, whatever the form of the greeting. Although the church carried the "holy kiss" into its liturgy, it is a greeting that does not need to be carried over into other cultures. As long as we greet each other as if we belonged to the same family, we capture the spirit of Paul's exhortation.

3. The Concern (v. 27).

"I charge you before the Lord to have this letter read to all the brothers."

Paul wasn't sure that his letter would be read to the entire congregation. The letter would be handed to the leaders of the church and the apostle wants to make sure that all the Thessalonians get to hear it. The apostle uses unusually strong language to enforce his request. He puts them under oath, as it were. This should, however, not be equated with the swearing which Jesus forbids in the Sermon on the Mount. No doubt the reading of the writings of the apostles in the churches played a major role in the formation of the New Testament canon of Scripture.

4. The Benediction (v. 28).

"The grace of our Lord Jesus Christ be with you."

The switch from the plural to the singular "I" in verse 27, suggests that Paul wrote these last words of his letter with his own hand. The letter began with grace and it ends with the grace of Jesus Christ. Salvation, ministry, holy living, and ultimate glory are all the gifts of divine grace.

The Spiritual Life of the Church

Personal Response

1. *How does Paul see the relationship between leaders and members in a congregation?*
2. *What suggestions are found in this passage for a ministry of the laity.*
3. *What significance did prayer have in Paul's thinking?*
4. *Are there any suggestions in our text on how we might improve our worship experiences?*

II THESSALONIANS

PRELIMINARY COMMENTS

A. The Relationship of the Two Letters to Each Other

The question has been asked why a person such as Paul, with his fertile mind, would write two letters to a church in which certain themes are repeated. On the other hand, there are such marked differences in eschatology, that scholars have wondered whether the same author produced both of these volumes. However, neither the similarities nor the differences are conclusive proof that Paul could not have written both of them.

Assuming that both epistles are from Paul's pen, scholars still ask the question: Why would the apostle write two letters to the same church so shortly after each other and how are we to explain the differences in tone and subject matter? One suggestion is that the Thessalonian church was divided into a Jewish and Gentile section, meeting separately. 1 Thessalonians, it is then said, was written to the

Gentile segment, and 2 Thessalonians to the Jewish church. However, it is hard for us to see how Paul would have acquiesced in such a situation. In fact we know nothing of a divided Thessalonian church.

Another suggestion is that one or the other of Paul's helpers (either Timothy or Silas) wrote one or the other of the letters. However, the style, the language and the theology of the letters is too much alike to make a convincing case against Pauline authorship.

Others have suggested that 2 Thessalonians was written before 1 Thessalonians. This is not inherently impossible since the letters of Paul as we now have them in our canon were ordered on the basis of length and so naturally the shorter one was called 2 Thessalonians. The traditional order of the two letters, however, makes good sense. 2 Thessalonians 2:14 makes reference to earlier correspondence, as does chapter 3:17. From that one can infer that an earlier epistle had already been sent to the Thessalonians. The slightly cooler tone of 2 Thessalonians can be explained by the interval between the two letters: the readers had evidently not taken Paul's admonitions in 1 Thessalonians sufficiently to heart and so the problems he addressed in his first letter have to be addressed once more and a bit more sharply.

Moreover, the personal reminiscences in the first letter are more natural than had they occurred in the second. Also, the added information on the *parousia* makes more sense in the light of Paul's teaching in 1 Thessalonians, than the other way round. For these and other reasons it seems best to follow the traditional order. We will take note of some of the similarities and differences in theology as we come to them.

Before we get into the letter we should observe that the salutation in 2 Thessalonians (1:1,2) is more or less the same as that of the first letter. Verse 1 is identical with 1 Thessalonians 1:1, "Silas and Timothy to the church of the Thessalonians in God our Father and the Lord Jesus Christ." The "our" before Father is not found in 1 Thessalonians 1:1.

The greeting (v. 2) is slightly longer in 2 Thessalonians: "Grace and peace to you from God the Father and the Lord Jesus Christ." This is the standard form of the greeting in Paul's letters. Although the addition "from God the Father and the Lord Jesus Christ" is missing in 1 Thessalonians it is implied. The Father and Son are closely linked together here as the source of grace and peace—blessings which Paul prays down upon his readers.

CHAPTER ONE

THE JUDGMENT AT CHRIST'S COMING

We ought always to thank God for you, brothers, and rightly so, because your faith is growing more and more, and the love every one of you has for each other is increasing. Therefore, among God's churches we boast about your perseverance and faith in all the persecutions and trials you are enduring. All this is evidence that God's judgment is right, and as a result you will be counted worthy of the kingdom of God, for which you are suffering. God is just: He will pay back trouble to those who trouble you and give relief to you who are troubled, and to us as well. This will happen when the Lord Jesus is revealed from heaven in blazing fire with his powerful angels. He will punish those who do not know God and do not obey the gospel of our Lord Jesus. They will be punished with everlasting destruction and shut out from the presence of the Lord and from the majesty of his power on the day he comes to be glorified in his holy people and to be marveled at among all those who have believed. This includes you, because you believed our testimony to you. With this in mind, we constantly pray for you, that our God may count you worthy of his calling, and that by his power he may fulfill every good purpose of yours and every act prompted by your faith. We pray this so that the name of our Lord Jesus may be glorified in you, and you in him, according to the grace of our God and the Lord Jesus Christ (2 Thess. 1:3-12).

Judgment is not the most palatable subject to write

about. We are told that D. L. Moody in his later years never spoke on this topic without weeping. The topic of judgment is so solemn and has about it mysteries which God has not seen fit to disclose, that we must approach it with modesty and humility. However, if we want to be true to the New Testament we can not avoid this teaching. Jesus and the apostles make it explicitly clear that it is appointed unto human beings once to die and after that comes the judgment. It is exegetically untenable to accept those passages which speak of the love and grace of God and to reject those which speak of judgment and wrath.

The judgments of God are revealed even now in history (Rom. 1:18). We see them in wars, revolutions, earthquakes, famines, plagues, political chaos, moral degradation and the hardening of people's hearts. These are however only forerunners of the judgment of God at the end of history. And in the passage that lies before us it is the final judgment that Paul has in mind.

I. Tribulation Prior to Christ's Coming (1:3-5).

Believers are not under the wrath of God. Jesus delivers them from God's wrath (1 Thess. 1:10). They have not been destined for wrath (1 Thess. 5:9) but to obtain salvation. That does not mean, however, that they are spared from suffering. Neither Jesus nor the apostles give us any guarantee that we will escape tribulation here on earth. Christians have suffered on account of their faith from the earliest days of the church up to the present. It is about these trials that Paul speaks in verses 3 to 5.

A. Growth in Spite of Suffering (v. 3).

"We ought always to thank God for you, brothers, and rightly so, because your faith is growing more and more, and the love every one of you has for each other is increasing."

Paul sees it as his Christian duty to thank God for the Thessalonians at all times. The word "ought" should not be read to suggest that Paul had failed in thanking God, and that he here confesses his shortcomings and reminds himself to be more faithful in the future. Nor does the word "ought" suggest that the apostle and his associates find it burdensome to thank God for their readers. It could be that after receiving the first letter in which Paul claims that he always thanks God for the Thessalonians, they had expressed feelings of unworthiness for such high honor. Paul now explains that such constant thanksgiving is altogether appropriate. What the word "ought" obviously does not mean is that there is little to be thankful for as he thinks of his readers, but since it is his Christian duty he will thank anyway.

The apostle addresses his readers as "brothers" at the very beginning of the letter, in order to underscore the personal relationship he has with the persecuted community. He and they are members of the family of God. And so it is only "fitting" that the apostles should thank God for them. Not only is it Paul's Christian duty to thank God for the Thessalonians, but they also deserve it; it is right and proper for him to do so. Paul has a sharp eye for what God was doing in the lives of his converts and he is not hesitant to speak words of commendation—something we are all too slow in doing.

Moreover, Paul has good reason to thank God: "Because your faith is growing more and more, and the love every one of you has for each other is increasing." In his first letter he thanks God for their faith and their love (1:3); here he is grateful that the readers are growing in these graces. Paul had prayed in his earlier letter that their love might grow (3:12; 4:10), and that prayer seems to have been answered.

Their faith is increasing beyond measure (*hyperauxano* occurs only here in the New Testament and is a compound belonging to Paul's many "hyper" words). The verb is in the present tense, suggesting that this growth is ongoing; it has not yet reached its ultimate goal. The word "faith" is not to be understood in the doctrinal sense of that word, but rather as a more comprehensive term for the Christian life. They are to become mature and strong Christians.

Practically a healthy Christian life shows itself in love for others, and Paul acknowledges also the increase in their love for each other. How would Paul have known? It must have been reported to him by word of mouth. What is amazing is that there was an increase of love in every one of the members for all the other members. We are often quite selective in our love for people; the Thessalonians embraced the entire Christian community with all of its weaknesses and faults. That calls for praise and commendation. Paul does not flatter his readers, but he does not withhold encouragement either. By directing his thanksgiving to God he spares them both pride and discouragement.

Having mentioned both faith and love, we might ask: what about the third member of that common Pauline triad, hope? The word itself does not occur in the context here but Paul does speak of endurance (v. 4) that springs from hope (as he puts it in 1 Thess. 1:3).

B. Steadfastness in Suffering (v. 4).

"Therefore, among God's churches we boast about your perseverance and faith in all the persecutions and trials you are enduring."

Paul is so impressed with the growth of the church and with its steadfastness under pressure that he and his associates boast about the Thessalonians in the churches—something that the founder of a church would perhaps not do ordinarily. He doesn't specify the churches in which he reported on the spiritual maturity of his readers; they are simply called "churches of God." Paul can also call them "churches of Christ" (Rom. 16:16) or "the churches of the saints" (1 Cor. 14:33).

The Thessalonians had endured steadfastly the many trials that came their way because they had accepted the gospel. The word "endurance" (*hupomone*) and "faith" are closely linked in our passage. One might understand "faith" to mean "faithfulness"; in that case it would not be too different from steadfastness or endurance. If, however, "faith" is understood in its usual sense of trust and commitment, then one might think of steadfastness as arising from the faith of the readers.

They have demonstrated steadfastness in "all persecutions and trials." The use of "all" shows that their sufferings had been many and varied. Two words are used to describe these trials: "persecutions" (*diogmos* in its verbal form means to pursue) and "afflictions" (*thlipsis* means pressure). These two words seem to be a word-pair which can be found elsewhere (e.g. Mark.4:17; Rom. 8:35), and are used here somewhat synonymously.

The readers are bearing up (*anecho* is in the present tense). They had received the gospel with much affliction (1 Thess. 1:6), and their sufferings had not yet let up. Paul had sent Timothy back to Thessalonica to strengthen the believers, lest they be shaken by the persecutions that came upon them (1 Thess. 3:2ff). No doubt Timothy's ministry contributed to the steadfastness of the Thessalonians. If Paul now boasts (the compound verb is found only here in the New Testament) in the strength of the faith of his converts, he is not contradicting his claim elsewhere that he will boast only in the cross of Jesus Christ (Gal. 6:14). He is not boasting in his own accomplishments. Rather, in the spirit of 1 Corinthians 1:31, Paul follows his own admonition: "Let the one who boasts, boast in the Lord."

C. Purpose in Suffering (v. 5).

"All this is evidence that God's judgment is right and as a result you will be counted worthy of the kingdom of God, for which you are suffering."

The connection of this verse with the previous one, is not clear. It could mean one of the following: steadfastness of the readers is evidence of God's righteous judgment; the persecution and affliction is the evidence; their endurance and faith in the face of persecution is the evidence of God's righteous judgment. The word *endeigma* (found only here in the New Testament) could mean either evidence, proof, or sign.

Perhaps Paul means that when innocent people suffer at the hands of the godless that is a sign that God will soon punish these evil-doers. By persecuting the Christians the enemies of the cross are exposed for what they really are, and God's righteous judgment will strike them in due time. Also, Jesus had promised to lead his followers to glory through suffering, and the suffering of the Thessalonians was a clear sign that the glory would follow. The trials and the fact that the readers are patiently enduring them is proof that God's judgments are righteous, for they make the saints worthy of glory.

Sufferings, patiently endured, make the believer worthy of the future kingdom of God. Or, to put it differently, their patient endurance of sufferings for the sake of the gospel demonstrates that they are worthy to enter the coming kingdom of God at the end of the age. "For which you also suffer," may suggest that Paul and his associates endure trials for the sake of the kingdom just as the Thessalonians do.

Having struck the note of judgment, Paul now goes on to describe the judgment of God on the wicked when Christ returns in glory.

II. Judgment at Christ's Coming (vv. 6-10).

A. The Nature of Divine Judgment (vv. 6-8).

First of all, there will be retribution. "God is just: He will pay back trouble to those who trouble you" (v. 6). Because God is just he will one day reverse the fortunes of both believers and the ungodly. At the moment it seems so unjust that innocent people should be persecuted for their faith. But God takes note and in due time he will repay the evil-doers (the verb *antapodidomi* is a double compound and conveys the notion of full and due requittal). Some modern readers think this strand of teaching is unchristian but, unpalatable though it might be, it is a fundamental teaching of the New Testament that God will recompense evil-doers—he will afflict those who afflict the saints with affliction.

Secondly, God's final judgment assures the saints their due reward: "And give relief to you who are troubled and to us as well" (v. 7a). God will give the suffering saints "rest" (*anesis* means relaxation; freedom from restraint). There is a rest for the people of God in the world to come (Heb. 4:9). Rest should not be understood as eternal inactivity but rather as rest from labors and trials, eschatological rest. Paul with his associates look forward to that rest as well, as the prepositional phrase "with us" so clearly indicates. The *parousia*, then, will be the occasion for both equitable retribution as well as for reward.

Thirdly, the judgment of God on the wicked is described as punishment. "This will happen when the Lord Jesus is revealed from heaven in blazing fire with his powerful angels. He will punish those who do not know God and do not obey the gospel of our Lord Jesus" (vv. 7b,8).

The *parousi*a of Christ is called the "revelation" in several New Testament texts (e.g. 1 Cor. 1:7). At the moment Christ is hidden from our eyes, but at his coming "every eye shall see him." Even though Christ is present with us by his Spirit, we walk by faith and not by sight. In the end, however, there will come a great unveiling. Christ's revelation at the end of human history is described with three prepositional phrases.

First, the revelation will be "from heaven." The singular "heaven" is used here rather than the more Semitic plural, as in 1 Thessalonians 1:10. When Christ ascended he went into heaven where he is highly exalted today at the right hand of God. At the end of this age he will come back from heaven, from the presence of God, as he promised his disciples (Acts 1:11).

Second, he will come with powerful angels or "angels of his power"—angels through whom he exercises his power. Jesus had promised that when the Son of Man returned in glory "all the angels" would be with him (Matt. 25:31). They are present at all the great events in the history of redemption. Third, he comes "in blazing fire." Fire is an important symbol of divine judgment. In Isaiah 66:15f. Yahweh is said to come in fire to execute judgment. In our text the image of the flaming fire portrays the frightening experience of the enemies of God on the day when God will inflict vengeance on them. God's punishment of the wicked is described as "vengeance:" "He will punish those who do not know God and do not obey the gospel of our Lord Jesus." Although *ekdikesis* can be translated simply as punishment, the context suggests that it is retributory punishment, and so "vengeance" is not an inappropriate translation. "Vengeance" should, however, not be understood as vindictiveness; it means that full justice will be inflicted on the evil-doers. And who are these evil-doers who will experience God's wrath in the end? Two groups of people are identified, but it looks as if we have here an example of synonymous parallelism. Those who do not know God and those who do not obey the gospel of our Lord Jesus refer to the same group of people, it seems. Those who do not know God are not the Gentiles who have never heard the gospel; rather, they are people who have refused to acknowledge God in their lives, and refused to obey the gospel. To disobey the gospel is another way of saying that they refused to believe in the good news. Paul has people in mind who willfully reject the knowledge of God (cf. Rom. 1:28) and the gospel of Christ. We may wonder at times just how God will judge those who have never heard the gospel, but we know that those who reject the gospel are under God's wrath.

B. The Consequences of Divine Judgment (vv. 9,10).

1. Eternal Destruction (v. 9).

"They will be punished with everlasting destruction and shut out from the presence of the Lord and from the majesty of his power."

The ungodly must pay the penalty of eternal destruction. Just as eternal life is the life of the age to come (Gal. 6:8), so is eternal destruction. The apostolic writers speak with restraint when it comes to this solemn truth, and do not define in detail what eternal punishment entails. But clearly death is not the extinction of the individual; all must appear before the Judge of all the earth. And we can be sure that he will judge justly.

Eternal destruction was for Paul synonymous with exclusion from the presence of the Lord. This kind of terminology is often found in the mouth of Jesus (Matt. 7:23; 8:12; 25:30,41). Eternal life means to see Christ's face (Rev. 22:4); eternal death means to be excluded from the city of God (Rev. 22:15). "The majesty of his power" is an example of synonymous parallelism. It elaborates on the meaning of the Lord's face, from which the ungodly will be excluded. To be shut out from the Lord's presence forever, means that the ungodly will experience the majesty of his power only as terror and not as blessing.

2. Eternal Glory (v. 10).

"On the day he comes to be glorified in his holy people and to be marveled at among all those who have believed."

Paul has no doubts that the Lord will come again at the end of the age, however, he makes no attempt to set dates. "Whenever he comes" is an indefinite temporal expression but raises no questions about the fact of the Lord's return.

When he comes he will "be glorifed in the saints." The saints are of course God's people. Although the word "saints" can also refer to angels, here it stands in parallel construction with "those who have believed." In contrast to those who have disobeyed the gospel (v. 8) stand those who have believed. And whereas the consequence of rejecting the gospel is eternal destruction, believers have the blessed hope of seeing Christ and sharing in his glory.

Christ, says Paul, will be glorified "in" his people. His glory will be seen in them, will be reflected in them. The preposition "in" could also be understood in the distributive sense of "among." Christ will be glorified in the midst of his saints. Also, he will be marvelled at. The saints, too, will be glorified, but here the emphasis is on the glorification of Christ by his redeemed people "on that day." And this glorious future is promised to the saints because they believed the testimony of the apostles. Paul calls his gospel a witness to the saving truths of Christ's work of redemption. He did not proclaim religious theories but witnessed to the salvatory acts of God in Christ. And to this witness the Thessalonians had responded in faith and now they can look forward to that great and glorious day of Christ's return.

III. Prayer in the Light of Christ's Coming (vv. 11,12).

A. The Content of the Prayer (v.11).

"With this in mind, we constantly pray for you, that our God may count you worthy of his calling, and that by his power he may fulfill every good purpose of yours and every act prompted by your faith" (v. 11).

In the light of Christ's coming in glory it is important that the readers live lives that are worthy of their calling. Paul and his associates pray that this purpose may in fact be fulfilled. This prayer for the Thessalonians is made not occasionally but "constantly." This word must not be understood in the absolute sense, as if the apostles never did anything else, but in the sense that it was very much a part of their everyday life. The word "also" may hark back to verse 3, where the thanksgiving of the apostles is mentioned. Here it is stated that they also pray. Or, perhaps the meaning is that the Thessalonians themselves are praying and Paul assures them that the apostles "also" pray.

One item of prayer for the readers is that they be counted worthy of their calling. As in verse 5, where we have the compound of the verb *axioō*, it is not clear whether we should translate "to be counted worthy" or "to be made worthy." In one sense, we suppose, believers could hardly be deemed worthy at Christ's coming if they were not made worthy.

To be worthy of their calling has nothing to do with a person's earthly career, profession or station in life. It has to do with the call of God in the gospel to which believers have responded. They are now to walk worthy of that calling (Eph. 4:1), worthy of the gospel (Phil. 1:27).

Another concern in the prayers of the apostles is that God might "fulfill every good purpose" and every act prompted by the faith of the readers. "To fulfill" means to bring the process to completion. Paul prays that God might complete every good resolve of the Thessalonians. The believer has a delight in well-doing, but often lacks the strength to carry out this resolve. Often we have to confess with Paul that the good that we want to do we fail to carry out (Rom. 7:15). We need divine enablement to carry out our good intentions.

A parallel to "good intentions" is the expression "work of faith." It refers to the efforts that spring from our faith in God (1 Thess. 1:3). "In power" indicates the power of God by which the believer is enabled to carry out the work that springs from a living faith and his resolve to do good. God's power is at work in the life of the believer through his Holy Spirit.

B. The Purpose (v. 12).

"We pray this so that the name of our Lord Jesus may be glorified in you, and you in him, according to the grace of our God and the Lord Jesus Christ" (v. 12).

Perhaps we could speak of the result of the prayer rather than the purpose, for if God enables his children to carry out their good resolves the name of the Lord Jesus will be glorified. Grammatically, however, we have here a purpose clause. The "name" in biblical thought stands for the person and so, when the name of Jesus is glorified, Christ himself is honored. Although in the context Paul has the *parousia* in mind, it is understood that the honoring of Christ's name takes place in the life of the believer in the present as well.

What is unique in our text is that the saints also are glorified. They will be glorified in union with Christ when he appears at the end of the age. However, this reciprocal process in which Christ is honored in the saints, and the saints are glorified in Christ, begins in this life (cf. 2 Cor. 3:18). All this is made possible only by the grace of God which has been extended to us by Jesus Christ our Lord. Grace is that unmerited kindness of God by which our salvation is made possible and the completion of the work that God has begun in the life of the believer.

Personal Response

1. On what basis could it be said (cf. v. 3) that someone's faith is growing?
2. How are the wrath of God and the grace of God related?
3. Christ's coming is called a "revelation" in verse 7. What other terms are used to describe Christ's return?
4. Christ's coming is described in 1 Thessalonians 4:14-18. What added features of this great event are found in our text?
5. What is the one condition that must be met if people are to escape God's final judgment (cf. v. 8 and v. 10)?
6. God, says Paul in Philippians 2:13, works in us both the willing and the doing. How is this illustrated in v. 11?

CHAPTER TWO

THE COMING OF THE LAWLESS ONE

Concerning the coming of our Lord Jesus Christ and our being gathered to him, we ask you, brothers, not to become easily unsettled or alarmed by some prophecy, report or letter supposed to have come from us, saying that the day of the Lord has already come. Don't let anyone deceive you in any way, for the day will not come, until the rebellion occurs and the man of lawlessness is revealed, the man doomed to destruction. He will oppose and will exalt himself over everything that is called God or is worshiped, so that he sets himself up in God's temple, proclaiming himself to be God. Don't you remember that when I was with you I used to tell you these things? And now you know what is holding him back, so that he may be revealed at the proper time. For the secret power of lawlessness is already at work; but the one who now holds it back will continue to do so till he is taken out of the way. And then the lawless one will be revealed, whom the Lord Jesus will overthrow with the breath of his mouth and destroy by the splendor of his coming. The coming of the lawless one will be in accordance with the work of Satan displayed in all kinds of counterfeit miracles, signs and wonders, and in every sort of evil that deceives those who are perishing. They perish because they refused to love the truth and so be saved. For this reason God sends them a powerful delusion so that they will believe the lie and so that all will be condemned who have not believed the truth but have delighted in wickedness (2 Thess. 2:1-12).

In the letters of John there are several references to Antichrist (1 John 2:18,22; 4:3; 2 John 7). "Anti," to begin with, meant "in the place of," but then came to mean also "against." There were antichrists (plural) in the first century (says John) as there are today. They oppose and hinder the work of Christ. However, John also predicts that at the end of history all opposition and rebellion against God and his Christ will be summed up in an evil personage, the Antichrist.

Similarly in the book of Revelation John portrays the Beast as waging war against Christ and his followers. These beastly powers arise out of the depths of evil from time to time throughout history. In the end, however, there will come a Beast who represents the epitome of evil and rebellion against God.

Paul does not use the same terminology but expresses the same idea. The sinister powers of lawlessness are at work today, as they were when Paul wrote. In the end, however, when Christ comes in glory, he will make an end of the "Man of Lawlessness," who incorporates in himself all the ungodliness and resistance to Christ's reign that has characterized this interim between the first and second coming of Christ. It is about this Lawless One that our text speaks—the only text in Paul where this aspect of eschatology is dealt with.

Before we get into this topic, let us take note of verses 1 and 2 which give us the background and occasion for Paul's instructions. "Concerning the coming of our Lord Jesus Christ and our being gathered to him, we ask you, brothers, not to become easily unsettled or alarmed by some prophecy, report or letter supposed to have come from us, saying that the day of the Lord has already come."

Paul begins this passage with a respectful request ("we ask you") and affectionate address ("brothers"). Evidently there were those who erroneously taught that the Lord had already come and this led to much confusion and even consternation in the ranks of the Thessalonians. Paul begs them now not to be shaken in their mind, not to lose their composure. The verb "unsettled is in the *aorist* and suggests the initial consternation; the verb "alarmed" is in the present tense, suggesting continuing nervous excitement.

The readers were distraught because of wrong teachings about the *parousia* of our Lord Jesus Christ. Paul has used this word repeatedly in 1 Thessalonians to designate the great event at the end of the age when Christ comes in glory. Although the word does not appear in 2 Thessalonians chapter 1, where he speaks of Christ's revelation (v. 7) and of "that day" (v.10), the *parousia* is meant.

When Christ comes at the end of the age the believers shall all be gathered to him. This concept has its roots in the Old Testament where God promises to gather the scattered exiles (Isa. 52:12) and it was then taken over by Jesus and the apostles to describe the gathering of the elect from the ends of the earth at the end of history (Mark 13:27; Matt. 23:37; Luke 13:34). Only here and in Hebrews 10:25 is the noun "gathering" (*episunagoge*) found in the New Testament. Although the writer to the Hebrews has the gathering of the saints for worship here on earth in mind, every gathering of the believers in Christ's name is a foretaste of the great gathering of the saints from the ends of the earth when Christ returns.

How did it happen that the Thessalonians got confused and nervous with respect to Christ's coming and the ingathering of the saints? Evidently some prophet had spoken "by the spirit" (or at least claimed he had) that the day of the Lord had already come. Paul had encouraged prophecy in the Thessalonian church (1 Thess. 5:19,20), but he had also urged them to test what the prophets said, particularly when they spoke about things yet to come.

The church historian Eusebius tells the story of a bishop in Pontus who had set a date for the return of Christ. The members of his congregation sold everything, stopped working, and waited prayerfully with fear and trembling for this great event to happen. They were all deeply disappointed.

Just what Paul means that the readers had become unsettled by "word" is not clear. Was it by a word of prophecy? Or was it a word of some preacher who did not claim to speak prophetically by the Spirit? Or was it a distortion of Paul's oral teachings which he had given the church before he left them?

Another channel of misinformation was "a letter." The phrase "as through us" possibly could go with "word" as well, but it certainly is connected with the word "epistle." This may suggest that someone had written a letter in the name of Paul and had stirred up the congregation. On the other hand, assuming the canonical order of the two Thessalonian letters, some people had misconstrued what Paul had written in his first letter and as a result people were losing their heads with respect to the *parousia.*

The rumor that had people in a flap was that the day of the Lord had already come. In that event they must have thought of the day of the Lord as a great day and that it had simply dawned, for they certainly knew from 1 Thessalonians and from Paul's oral teachings that the great cosmic event, the coming of Christ at the end of the age, had not yet taken place. Some translators prefer to render the verb *enistemi* (to stand, to be present) as "at hand" or "to be imminent." In any case they were distressed by an over-realized eschatology which some evidently were propounding.

From this brief introduction of the topic; the coming of the Lawless One, we can see that waiting for the Lord's return should not lead to nervous excitement. Rather it should motivate believers to live holy lives and to fulfill their calling here on earth. Incidentally, it should be noticed, that Christians are nowhere encouraged to wait for Antichrist. He will come in due time, but we should not constantly be picking candidates.

I. The Revelation of the Lawless One (vv. 3-7).

A. The Time of His Revelation (v. 3).

"Don't let anyone deceive you in any way, for the day will not come, until the rebellion occurs and the man of lawlessness is revealed, the man doomed to destruction."

"The day" is shorthand for "the day of the Lord," mentioned in verse 2, and is another way of designating the *parousia*, as can be seen quite readily from 1 Thessalonians 5:1,2. The day which marks the end of this present age will not come, says Paul, until the rebellion occurs. The word for rebellion in Greek is *apostasia* (from which our word apostasy is derived). It was a word used for military or political rebellions. Satan is at work to bring about a widespread, utter defiance of God and his kingdom before our Lord returns.

It does not follow, of course, that it will be possible to set a date for the Lord's return by the degree of wickedness that this world is yet to witness. Christ will still come "as a thief in the night" (1 Thess. 5:2). In the New Testament generally it is felt that before the last day comes there is going to be a great increase in religious apostasy, immorality and wickedness of every sort. To infer from Paul's words that there will be a Jewish apostasy before our Lord comes or that perhaps a great number of believers will fall away from the Lord is unwise. The meaning seems to be that there will generally be a great build-up of evil before this age comes to an end.

The Thessalonians were being led astray by those who insisted that the end had already dawned, and Paul warns them not to be deceived. Jesus had said something similar: "Take heed that no one leads you astray" (Mark 13:5).

The prime mover of this final rebellion against God is the man of lawlessness (some manuscripts read "man of sin"), the son of perdition. "Man of lawlessness" and "son of perdition" are Semitic expressions in which one noun is used to describe another. This lawless person is destined for destruction, perdition, hell (the same expression designates Judas in John 17:8). Although Paul does not use the word, he undoubtedly means what John means with Antichrist.

The son of lawlessness should not be identified simply with Satan himself (notice that in v. 9 the two are clearly held apart). Nor should one think of him only as the personification of evil. And certainly it would be unwise to say that the Roman caesars, who persecuted the church, were antichrists, even though they were beastly, as John in the Revelation indicates. At the time of the Reformation the pope was regularly identified as the man of sin by Protestant opponents, and it cannot be denied that when the Roman church persecuted true believers there was something profoundly antichristian about it. Also, we should not identify evil personages in our day as "the" antichrist. Evil monsters, like Hitler and Stalin, may have seemed to people in their day as good candidates, but clearly they were not the antichrist, the man of lawlessness. It is best, we think, to interpret Paul to say that at the end of this age an eschatological personage who incorporates in himself the great rebellion of fallen humanity against God, will appear.

Before Christ comes this man of lawlessness will be "revealed." Just as Christ's coming is called a revelation (v. 7), so Antichrist is to have a revelation, meaning, he will appear. That may mean that he will be at work some time before the *parousia*, but will be made manifest only when Christ comes.

Although we appreciate all the progress that humankind has made in so many areas (medicine, communication, technology), the teaching about antichrist clearly shows the dark line in human history. Instead of the human race getting better and better, history ends with the manifestation of evil of awesome proportions. Of course, that is not the end of the story, for the man of lawlessness is doomed; he goes to destruction.

B. The Nature of the Rebellion (v. 4).

"He will oppose and will exalt himself over everything that is called God or is worshiped, so that he sets himself up in God's temple, proclaiming himself to be God."

The language of this verse reminds us of Daniel 11:36,37, where Antiochus IV is depicted as an enemy of God. Antichrist is an adversary, an opposer (*antikeimenos*). Active, relentless hostility to God and his people is implied. A second participle describes the man of lawlessness as arrogant: he exalts himself over everything called God or an object of worship. The present tense of the two participles indicates a continuing attitude. He demands religious veneration. No god or anything bearing God's name, nor any object of worship (images, shrines, altars) is permitted to overshadow this evil personage. He must be first of all. He is, one might say, a thorough going secularist, who opposes everything that people hold sacred.

His goal is totalitarianism. He sets himself up in God's temple proclaiming himself to be God. Violation of the temple in Jerusalem provides the background for this kind of terminology. Antiochus Epiphanes (168 BC) had defiled the temple, as had the Roman general Pompey (63 BC). And in AD 40 Caligula ordered that his image be placed in the temple in Jerusalem (he died before the order was carried out).

Just what specifically is meant by this prophecy of Antichrist's rule is not certain. Some Bible readers infer from our text that some day before the Lord returns the temple in Jerusalem will be rebuilt and that the man of lawlessness will literally seek to rule the world from this new temple. But the New Testament knows nothing of a rebuilt temple. Jesus predicted only its destruction. It had had its day; sacrifices were no longer called for after Christ sacrificed himself. The church is now the temple of God (I Cor. 3:16).

Since the church is described as the temple of God some commentators then argue that Antichrist will find his place in an apostate church. But we have no reason to believe that the church at the end of the age will be so corrupt that it will invite the man of sin into its midst. Others suggest that the destruction of the Jerusalem temple in AD 70 was the fulfilment of this prediction, but surely that event cannot be identified with the revelation of the man of lawlessness.

It is best to understand Paul's language as metaphorical. It is a way of saying that this evil person defiantly and arrogantly claims to be God. The temple of God may in fact be a reference to God's heavenly dwelling place and Antichrist usurps the authority of God, proclaiming himself to be God.

C. The Restraint on His Manifestation (vv.5-7).

"Don't you remember that when I was with you I used to tell you these things? And now you know what is holding him back, so that he may be revealed at the proper time. For the secret power of lawlessness is already at work; but the one who now holds it back will continue to do so till he is taken out of the way."

From verse 5 it is obvious that Paul had included some instruction about the eschatological rebellion and its evil leader. For this reason Paul does not give us too many details. We are often left guessing as to what he meant specifically. It should be noted that whereas the apostle uses the plural throughout the letter, here he reverts to the singular "I." There seems to be a slight criticism of the readers in this verse. They had not remembered what Paul had repeatedly (*eleqon* is in the imperfect) said about these events that characterize the wrap-up of this age.

Verse 6 suggests that the readers had been told what it is that restrains the manifestation of the man of lawlessness. The participle *katechon* (to hold down, hold back) is in the neuter in verse 6, but in verse 5 it is in the masculine. That makes it even more difficult to identify what or who does the restraining.

A great many suggestions have been made as to who this restraining force (or person) might be: (a) The Roman empire, with its law and order, is one possibility. The masculine participle would then point to the emperor and the neuter to the Roman state. Certainly Paul had experienced the protection of the Roman authorities in his ministry. (b) Paul and the preaching of the gospel has also been suggested. But would Paul speak of himself so cryptically? Besides, did he really think that his missionary activity kept the Antichrist from manifesting himself? (c) The Holy Spirit and the work of the church have also been suggested. He who restrains would then be the Holy Spirit and that which restrains the church in which the Spirit is at work. It is assumed in this line of thought that the Holy Spirit's activity ceases when the church has reached completion at the coming of Christ, and with the Spirit and the church out of the way, Antichrist has free rein. But we do not really have any grounds for holding that the church will be removed before the man of lawlessness appears.

George Ladd has suggested that God himself is the Restrainer. But how can it be said that he will be put out of the way (v. 7)? Ladd takes "the one is taken out of the way" to be a reference to Antichrist.

It is even possible that the verb *katecho* has a different meaning in our text than "restrain." What if it were translated "to hold power"? In that case the one who holds sway today might be thought of as Satan. Paul is then not speaking of any restraining power, that holds Antichrist's revelation in check, but speaks of the demonic power of evil that is at work today and which finds its climax in the man of lawlessness.

"So that he may be revealed at the proper time," implies that ultimately God is in control and only when God's hour strikes will this evil personage become manifest. God restrains evil in a variety of ways (by the Holy Spirit, the church, the state, angelic beings, and so forth), but when this age has run its course, and the mission of the church is complete, God lifts all restraints and a fierce rebellion against God will occur.

The stirrings of that rebellion could be seen already in the first century. "For the secret power of lawlessness is already at work." The word "mystery" does not mean that evil is at work in secret (although it often is). Ordinarily the word refers to something in the salvatory purposes of God that was hidden from the eyes of humans in the past but that has been revealed now through Jesus Christ. In our text there may be a reference to the fact that we cannot understand the depths of wickedness and rebellion against God unless God opens our eyes. Today people often look for the explanation for the awful acts of violence and sexual crimes in our society without acknowledging that there are demonic powers at work in our fallen humanity. Evil continues to "work" (regularly used for super-human activity) until it reaches its apex at the end of history. At the moment evil is under restraint. But some day the restrainer (or is it the man of lawlessness?) will be removed and then evil will be seen in all its glaring ugliness.

II. The Destruction of the Lawless One (v. 8).

"And then the lawless one will be revealed, whom the Lord Jesus will overthrow with the breath of his mouth and destroy by the splendor of his coming."

Once the restrainer has been removed the lawless one will be revealed. This sets the stage for the manifestation of wickedness in all of its ghastly forms, but it also indicates that the end of this age has arrived. For when this evil personage will finally be revealed he will be destroyed by Christ when he comes in his glory. Just how long the Antichrist will be allowed to do his evil work is not stated, but his demise is certain.

Christ, who is appropriately called "Lord" in our text, will destroy the lawless one with the breath of his mouth (language that is found in Isa. 11:4). Not even an action on the part of Christ seems to be necessary. By his coming

Christ puts Antichrist out of commission. The verb *katargeo* means literally "to render idle" and comes to mean to "nullify" or "put out of work." (It occurs 27 times in the New Testament and the Authorized Version renders it by 17 different words. That simply illustrates the difficulty of translating this verb.)

The Lord's coming is regularly called his *"parousia."* In our text, however, we have the unusual expression: the *epiphaneia* (appearing) of his *parousia* (coming). *"Epiphaneia* is found only here outside the Pastoral Epistles. Paul seems to be piling up words to describe Christ's glorious appearing which will make an end of Antichrist and his rule. John Darby taught that *parousia* referred to Christ's coming before the tribulation and *epinhaneia* his coming after the tribulation, but grammatically that is untenable. Moreover, there is nothing in the New Testament that suggests that the church will be spared tribulation or will be raptured before the last tribulation strikes.

Although Paul has already taken us to the end of history when the man of lawlessness will be slain by the coming of our Lord, he now backs up and gives us a few glimpses of the sinister activities of this evil personage.

III. The Deceitful Activity of the Lawless One (vv. 9-12)

A. His Satanic Inspiration (vv. 9,10).

"The coming of the lawless one will be in accordance with the work of Satan displayed in all kinds of counterfeit miracles, signs and wonders, and in every sort of evil that deceives those who are perishing. They perish because they refused to love the truth and so be saved."

This false Christ has his *parousia*, too. The word is probably used as a parody of Christ's *parousia* in the previous verse. Antichrist's coming is according to the *energeia* (energizing) of Satan. Satan is the Semitic word for the

Greek word "devil" (*diabolos*). This reminds us of the Beast in the Revelation who gets his authority from the Dragon (Rev. 13: 2) The man of lawlessness is empowered by Satan to do Satan's work.

With powers and signs and wonders—words used to describe the miracles of Christ—Antichrist deceives people. The false prophet who, in the Revelation, is the Beast's propaganda minister, also does great signs in order to get people to worship the Beast (Rev. 13). Jesus warned his disciples against such false Christs who would lead people astray by signs and wonders (Mark 13:22; Matt. 24:24).

When it is said that these powerful deeds of this evil personage are "false", Paul is not questioning their reality, but he is saying that they are done in a spirit of falsehood. Antichrist's coming and his activity will be such a clever parody of Christ's coming that many will be carried away.

His activity will be characterized by wicked deception. He is out to lure people to their destruction. Of the Beast, in Revelation 13, it is said that he deceives the earth dwellers (said to be those whose names are not written in the Lamb's book of life, 13:8). Here, too, it is those perishing that are deceived. Those who remain loyal to Jesus are protected.

The reason people are deceived by this evil personage, says Paul, is "they received not the love of the truth, that they might be saved." God wants all people to be saved and to come to the knowledge of the truth (1 Tim. 2:4), but when people reject the truth they forfeit the means of salvation. The truth is, of course, God's revelation; it is the truth of the gospel of Christ, who is the way, the truth and the life (John 14:6).

The truth of the gospel must be received, welcomed, embraced. It must be loved. When people refuse to do that, they cannot be saved.

B. His Disastrous Success (vv. 11,12).

"For this reason God sends them a powerful delusion

so that they will believe the lie and so that all will be condemned who have not believed the truth but have delighted in wickedness."

It's because they refused the truth that God sends them a "working (*enerqeia*) of delusion." *Energeia* suggests a superhuman power is set in motion which makes unbelievers prone to embrace the lie. This is a process of judicial blinding. We have a parallel in Romans 1:21-28, where divine judgment is seen in giving people over to more wickedness because they suppressed the truth. People who reject the gospel voluntarily, in the end reach the stage when they can no longer tell what is gospel and what is fallacy. This is the powerful delusion which Paul here describes as an act of God. When people refuse the truth God sends the working of error. This is happening today but evidently will take place on a grand scale at the end of the age.

Those who "exchange the truth for the lie" (Rom. 1:25) have no other prospect but the judgment of God. In verse 10 Paul speaks of those who refuse to receive the truth; here he uses a parallel phrase: "they have not believed the truth." And the opposite of believing the truth is to delight in wickedness. For those who are deceived by the man of lawlessness, who work by the inspiration of Satan, there is no hope for the future, only the judgment of God, eternal punishment.

Personal Response

1. *In what kind of spirit ought we to wait for the return of our Lord (vv. 1,2)?*
2. *If there is to be a climax in the manifestation of evil at the end of the age, what should be our attitude with respect to efforts to improve life here on earth?*
3. *Antichrist is coming, says John, and there are already many antichrists. How does that jive with what Paul says in our text about the coming of the lawless one?*
4. *We are exhorted to wait for the Savior's return. Do we have any en-*

couragement in the New Testament to be on the look-out for Antichrist?
5. *How can we be kept from being deceived by evil powers (v. 10)?*
6. *Is there any connection between holding to the truth and morals (cf. v. 12)?*

CHAPTER THREE

EXHORTATION TO STEADFASTNESS

> *But we ought always to thank God for you, brothers loved by the Lord, because from the beginning God chose you to be saved through the sanctifying work of the Spirit and through belief in the truth. He called you to this through our gospel, that you might share in the glory of our Lord Jesus Christ. So then, brothers, stand firm and hold to the teachings we passed on to you, whether by word of mouth or by letter. May our Lord Jesus Christ himself and God our Father, who loved us and by his grace gave us eternal encouragement and good hope, encourage your hearts and strengthen you in every good deed and word (2 Thess 2:13-17).*

The exhortation to stand firm is heard in all the books of the New Testament. From the mouth of Jesus and the apostles, whose writings now form the New Testament canon, comes constant encouragement to be steadfast. The reason for such admonitions is not hard to find: Christians right from the beginning when the church was established were under attack.

The call to steadfastness should not be understood to mean that believers are to be inflexible. The ability to adapt to new situations is a strength rather than a weakness. However, the followers of Jesus must not compromise the basic tenets of the gospel. Also, they must give their supreme loyalty to Christ as their Lord and never waver in their commitment to the one who redeemed them at great cost.

Besides persecution, the early church was threatened by false teachings, and so the call to stand firm is also an encouragement to hold firmly to the faith "that God has once for all entrusted to the saints" (Jude 3). Moreover, Christians were also exposed to temptations of various sorts, and so they are exhorted to stand firm in their conflict with the world, the flesh and the devil.

The Thessalonians had been upset by wrong teachings concerning the coming of Christ (v. 2). Paul wants them to be sober and clear-headed and to stand firm and not be shaken in their commitment to Christ and his kingdom. The following paragraph represents Paul's call to steadfastness.

I. The Foundation for Steadfastness (vv. 13,14).

A. Divine Election (v. 13).

"But we ought always to thank God for you, brothers loved by the Lord, because from the beginning God chose you to be saved through the sanctifying work of the Spirit and through belief in the truth."

For the second time in this letter Paul says that he and his friends are obligated to thank God for the Thessalonians (cf. 1:3). He cannot help but give thanks to God for their Christian state. Again he addresses them affectionately as "brothers" but adds a participle in the perfect tense "beloved." They have been loved and are still loved by the Lord. And, as in 1 Thessalonians 1:4, where the fact that they are loved by God is connected with election, so also here.

God has chosen them from the beginning. The word "to choose" is one of several words used to express the idea of election. Salvation has its origin in God's grace and not in human endeavors. Instead of the phrase "from the beginning" some good manuscripts read "as first-fruits." Although that is not an uncommon term in Paul, the context seems to favor "from the beginning." In that event the meaning is probably similar to Ephesians 1:4, where election is said to have taken place before the foundation of the world.

God chose the readers (and us) for salvation (not for

wrath, cf. 1 Thess. 5:9). Salvation (deliverance) stands here in marked contrast to the destruction that awaits those who reject the truth (v. 10). How was the salvation of the Thessalonians brought about? By the "sanctification of the Spirit." The spirit (*pneuma*) is not the human spirit that is sanctified (although it may well be) but rather it is the Spirit of God that does the sanctifying. By God's Spirit the whole person is sanctified (1 Thess. 5:23; cf. also 1 Pet. 1:2). Perhaps it should be pointed out that all three members of the trinity are mentioned in our verse.

Whereas election stresses the divine initiative in our salvation, and the Holy Spirit makes election a reality in our lives, this does not happen without our response to the gospel: "by the belief of the truth." The truth is again the revelation of God found in the gospel.

B. Divine Calling (v. 14).

"He called you to this through our gospel, that you might share in the glory of our Lord Jesus Christ."

God's purpose for his children is that they should experience salvation in all its fullness, beginning here on earth and culminating in God's eternal kingdom. For this purpose he called us. Election and calling run closely parallel to each other in meaning. He chose us in eternity; he called us through the gospel. In 1 Thessalonians 2:12 and 5:24 the tense of the verb to call is present; here it is *aorist*, a past tense. This points to the time when the readers responded to the gospel in faith and obedience and committed their lives to Christ. What Paul calls "our gospel" is nothing other than the gospel of Jesus Christ (cf. 1 Thess. 1:5,8).

God called us so that we might share in the glory of our Lord Jesus Christ. Paul began with election in eternity past; he spoke of the call of the gospel in time; and now he takes us into the future where eternal glory awaits the believer. The salvation for which the believers have been chosen is not only a present experience but it has a futuristic aspect: obtaining glory. To share the glory of God is one of the most common ways of describing the final destiny of the people of God. Jesus prayed (John 17:24) that his followers might see his glory which he had before the world began. Glory expresses the essence of all eschatological hopes of the believer.

II. The Nature of Steadfastness (v. 15).

"So then, brothers, stand firm and hold to the teachings we passed on to you, whether by word of mouth or by letter."

This verse begins with two inferential particles "so, then." Again he addresses his readers affectionately as brothers (and sisters). One might have thought since God had chosen the Thessalonians from eternity and called them through the gospel to obtain the glory of our Lord Jesus Christ, that they might now relax. However, Paul calls on them to stand firm. Only if they remain steadfast can Paul truly live (1 Thess. 3:8). The verb is in the present imperative and indicates that this is something that must go on. They must keep on planting their feet firmly on the ground. Implied in the command to stand firm is the fact that there is opposition and danger.

A second command is an exhortation to hold fast to the traditions. To have a firm grip on the "traditions" means to have a firm grasp of the teachings of the apostles. The word "tradition" today has a negative ring about it. In the Gospels it is frequently used for Jewish practices that stood over against the Scriptures. However, the word is often used in a positive sense as well. Apostolic teaching that is passed on to others is called "tradition." In 1 Corinthians 11:2 Paul commends his readers for maintaining the traditions he had passed on to them. Traditions describe the living faith of those who have preceded us; traditionalism describes the dead faith of the living.

The traditions which the Thessalonians had been taught came to them both orally ("by word") or in written form ("by letter"). The one is as authoritative as the other. The word of God can be taught both orally and in writing. The letter by which they had been taught the traditions is very likely a reference to 1 Thessalonians.

There are some good traditions which the church over a long period of time has built up on the apostolic traditions; others are not so good. Apostolic traditions must be faithfully adhered to; church traditions should be carefully evaluated and those which have been tested and found helpful followed; others might be left behind.

III. The Prayer for Steadfastness (vv. 16,17)

A. The Address (v. 16a).

"May our Lord Jesus Christ himself and God our Father."

Paul has exhorted his readers, but he knows very well that in their own strength they won't accomplish very much so he directs them to the source of all strength. And just as chapter 1 closed with a prayer, so does our second chapter. There are at least two more prayers in this short letter which indicates how significant intercessary prayer was in the life of the apostle.

He addresses his prayer, first of all, to Christ, giving him his full name: "Our Lord Jesus Christ." Just as in 1 Thessalonians 1:1 and 3:11, Paul couples the Father and the Son. What is interesting is that he puts Christ's name before the Father's. Twenty years after the resurrection of Jesus, Christians are addressing prayers to him and putting him on the same level as God.

God is addressed as "Father"—something Jesus taught his disciples. Jewish rabbis cautioned against this kind of intimacy, but Christians had no inhibitions about addressing God as Father, for Jesus had revealed the Father by his coming. As long as God's people can speak to God as their Father they can live with the mysteries and tragedies of life, for they know that their lives are in the hands of a loving God.

B. The Encouragement (v. 16b).

"Who loved us and by his grace gave us eternal encouragement and good hope."

"The one who loved us" could refer either to Christ or God or both. God's love was seen in choosing us for salvation; it was supremely manifested in the sacrifice of his Son. The past tense ("loved") probably points to the climax of God's (and Christ's) love: the cross.

His love manifested itself, among other things, in giving us eternal comfort. *Paraklesis* can also be translated as encouragement, strength, help, exhortation, and so forth. If we take the original meaning of the English word "comfort," namely that of strength, then perhaps encouragement or strengthening would be an appropriate rendering here. But in what sense is this *paraklesis* eternal? Does he mean that it is not transitory or that it does not fail? Perhaps, but more likely the meaning is that it begins here and lasts for all eternity.

Not only has God and Christ given us good comfort but also "good hope." Romans 15:4 also combines comfort with hope. Since the comfort is eternal the meaning is not too different from hope itself. In Titus 2:13 Paul speaks of a blessed hope; Peter writes of a living hope (1 Pet. 1:3). Here we have "a good hope." The early Christians often lived under difficult circumstances, but they were sustained by hope. This was not simply wishful thinking. Hope is rather more concrete in the New Testament than the word is in our everyday usage. It is a hope laid up in heaven (Col. 1:5).

This eternal comfort and good hope are gifts of God's grace. Everything we have is attributed by Paul to the unmerited goodness and kindness of God, who came to us in Jesus Christ.

C. The Content (v. 17).

"Encourage your hearts and strengthen you in every good deed and word."

First of all Paul prays to God that he might strengthen (*parakaleo*) the hearts of his readers. The heart stands for the whole inner person and Paul's wish-prayer for the Thessalonians is that they might be given the fortitude to stand firm in the trials and temptations to which they were exposed. A second wish-prayer is that God might establish or strengthen them in every good deed and word. If "hearts" has the inner being in focus, "good deed and word" stresses the outer expressions of the Christian life. Paul's concern is that inward encouragement in the face of external opposition be accompanied by behavior that is fitting for the saints. The two verbs in our verse ("strengthen" and "establish") are found as a word pair also in 1 Thessalonians 3:2, where Paul explains that his purpose in sending Timothy was to establish and strengthen them in their faith. The collocation of "work" and "word" is found in several other passages (cf. Luke 24:19; Acts 7:22). Here the adjective "good" is added—the kind of deeds and words that one expects from followers of Christ.

Personal Response

1. How is the divine initiative and the human response combined in verse 13?
2. When and how did you first hear the call of the gospel (v. 14)?
3. How would standing firm express itself in our day and age (v. 15)?
4. What does "holding to the traditions" mean for us today (v. 15)?
5. How do we experience the strengthening of our hearts (v. 17)?
6. What place to good works and words have in the Christian life (v. 17)?

CHAPTER FOUR

A PRAYER FOR MISSION

Finally, brothers, pray for us that the message of the Lord may spread rapidly and be honored, just as it was with you. And pray that we may be delivered from wicked and evil men, for not everyone has faith. But the Lord is faithful, and he will strengthen and protect you from the evil one. We have confidence in the Lord that you are doing and will continue to do the things we command. May the Lord direct your hearts into God's love and Christ's perseverance (2 Thess. 3:1-5).

Our passage begins with *to loipon*, which means quite literally "as for the rest." Sometimes this expression indicates a change of subject, at other times it suggests that the writer is drawing his letter to a close. In our passage it also marks a change to the more hortatory part of the letter.

We have already noticed that Paul expresses wish-prayers for his readers here and there in this letter. Now, however, he asks the Thessalonians to pray for him. Paul was a man of great ability but he never trusted in his own gifts to do the work of the Lord; he lived in complete dependence on God. For that reason he does not find it beneath his dignity to ask his fellow Christians to pray for him and his colleagues.

I. The Request for Prayer (vv. 1,2).

A. For the Spread of the Gospel (v. 1).

"Finally, brothers, pray for us that the message of the Lord may spread rapidly and be honored."

In 1 Thessalonians 5:25 the request for prayer was general; here it is more specific. There are two matters in particular that Paul asks his readers to pray for: one, that the word of the Lord might run. The verb to pray (*proseuchomai*) is in the present imperative and the thought is that they are to keep on praying for the spread of the gospel. Repeatedly in his letters Paul asks the churches to uphold the witness of the apostles in their prayers (cf. Eph. 6:19,20; Col. 4:3,4).

The gospel is called "the word of the Lord" (as in 1 Thess. 1:8). It is a message about the Lord Jesus, but also it is a proclamation that comes from him; it is not simply the product of human reflection. Sometimes Paul speaks of himself as a runner in the race (e.g. 1 Cor. 9:24) but here he asks them to pray that the gospel message itself might run. Paul is a master at vivid figures of speech. Did he think of the runners at the Isthmian or Olympic games when he wrote this line, or was Ps. 147:15 in his mind, where it is stated that God's word runs quickly? When God's word runs the good news is spread.

But what does it mean that the word of the Lord "be glorified?" If the metaphor of the runner is still in Paul's mind then perhaps the meaning is that the word of the Lord triumph; that it be crowned at the finish line. And how is it crowned? When the gospel is received and people are saved. When Paul and Barnabas preached the gospel at Antioch of Pisidia and people received the message, Luke tells us that they "were glad and glorified the word of the Lord" (Acts 13:48).

Earlier in this letter the apostle spoke of the persecution believers had to endure at the present, prior to the coming of the Lord. Jesus had predicted that (Mark 13:9,11). However, Jesus foresaw also that the gospel would be preached to all nations before the end came (Mark 13:10), and Paul asks his readers to pray that the gospel which Paul proclaimed might spread and that people everywhere might receive it. In this way the word of the Lord would be honored. He reminds his readers once more of how the word had come to them and how they had received it ("just as it was with you").

B. For the Safety of the Messengers (v. 2).

"And pray that we may be delivered from wicked and evil men, for not everyone has faith."

In 1 Thessalonians 1:10 the verb "deliver" was used for being saved from divine wrath; here the same verb is used for deliverance from evil people. In Romans 15:31 he asks the Roman Christians to pray for him that he might be delivered from the unbelievers in Judea. Precisely who the opponents of the gospel were, from whom he now wants to be delivered, is not stated. Since he is writing from Corinth he may have had the Jewish antagonists in mind.

He describes these enemies of the Christian faith as *atopoi* (literally "out of place"). English versions render that word as "unreasonable" (AV), "bigoted" (JB), "wicked" (NRSV) and so forth. Since it is joined with the adjective "evil" it shares in its meaning. These opponents of the gospel are "out of place" in an ethical sense.

To be rescued from evil people does not mean that he did not want to have anything to do with them, for he wanted all people to hear the gospel and be saved. But repeatedly the enemies of the gospel had interferred with his mission—he was beaten, imprisoned, dragged before magistrates and suffered numerous other indignities. Paul was quite willing to suffer for the sake of the gospel, but he knows, too, that the gospel cannot run and be glorified if those who oppose the good news constantly put road-blocks in the way.

"Not everyone has faith" is probably Paul's explanation of why there are opponents to his mission. Not everyone accepts the gospel; they persist in unbelief. "Faith" here is not so much a body of beliefs but as we say "the Christian faith," faith in Jesus as Savior and Lord. The opposition Paul was concerned about came from people outside the church.

In contrast to those who refuse to embrace the Christian faith is the Lord who is faithful, and he will keep the Thessalonians from the evil one.

II. The Assurance of Divine Protection (v. 3).

"But the Lord is faithful, and he will strengthen and protect you from the evil one."

There appears to be a deliberate play on words here: in contrast to those without faith, the Lord is faithful (*pistis*— faith, *pistos*— faithful). Not the might of the enemy is uppermost in Paul's mind but the faithfulness of Christ. More frequently Paul speaks of the faithfulness of God (I Cor. 1:9; 10:13; 2 Cor. 1:18), but here he has Christ, the Lord, in mind.

How does this faithfulness manifest itself in the life of his children? "He will strengthen and protect you from the evil one." In chapter 2:17 the apostle prayed that God would strengthen and establish his readers; here he assures them that he will. If the verb "to strengthen" speaks of inner fortification, then the verb "to guard" implies the outer working of God's providence.

The assurance that Christ will guard the Thessalonians from the evil one is reminiscent of the Lord's Prayer in which we have the petition: "Deliver us from the evil one." It is hard to say whether one should render the adjective with the article as "the evil one" (masculine) or "the evil" (neuter) in the Lord's Prayer as well as in our text. No doubt behind the evil people from whom Paul wants to be rescued, stands the evil one, Satan, for he uses people to hinder the ongoing work of the kingdom.

In the mission of church, then, there are superhuman dimensions that are not always sufficiently recognized. There is the God who has promised that his word shall not return empty, but there is also the Devil who constantly seeks to ruin God's work. As witnesses of the gospel, then, we are involved in a spiritual warfare, and must, therefore, look to spiritual resources. One of these is prayer, and Paul recognizes the significance of prayer in his calling.

III. The Confidence in the Readers (v. 4)

"We have confidnece in the Lord that you are doing and will continue to do the things we command."

As a wise teacher Paul expresses confidence in his converts. His confidence rests, however, not simply in the character of the readers, but "in the Lord." He commends them for doing that which he and his associates had commanded and expects them to keep on in this manner.

The word "command" has a martial ring to it, for it was used in the military for officers commanding their troops. Five times in the following verses is the language of command used. The word is used for ethical and ecclesiastical instruction. The commands he has in mind are probably the instructions he gave the Thessalonians when he established the church. Included in these commands would also be the instructions found in Paul's first letter to the Thessalonians.

In a moment Paul will give them new instructions and so it is tactful on his part to commend them for their obedient response to apostolic teaching up to this point. People respond more readily to instruction when the teacher expresses confidence that the instructions will be carried out. From that point of view Paul was a wise pastor.

IV. The Prayer for the Thessalonians (v. 5).

"May the Lord direct your hearts into God's love and Christ's perseverence."

Here we have another wish-prayer which Paul utters from time to time as he writes his letters. We have the verb "to direct" in I Thessalonians 3:11, where, it was used more literally for the opening up of a way so that Paul might visit his recent converts. In our passage the verb is used metaphorically for directing the hearts of the readers. "Inclining the heart" is a well-known Old Testament phrase (cf. 1 Chron. 29:18; 2 Chron. 12:14). Only once more is this verb found in the New Testament and that is in Luke 1:79 where the hope is expressed that the coming one will guide people's feet in the ways of peace.

Although Paul has expressed full confidence in the obedience of his readers, he knows that only God can create in them the willingness and the strength to respond positively to the teachings of the apostles. And for this reason he prays that their hearts might be directed to the "love of God." If this is an objective genitive, then it is their love for God that Paul is concerned about. On the other hand, a subjective genitive would be the love of God for the readers. Another possibility is that Paul prays that their hearts might be directed to "divine" love (descriptive genitive), meaning that they are to love the way God loves. It is not impossible that Paul was consciously imprecise so that all of these aspects might be included. It is a well-known fact in Christian experience that when believers meditate deeply on the love God has shown them in Jesus Christ, that they respond spontaneously in love and obedience to God.

But what does it mean to direct the heart to the "endurance of Christ"? Does he mean that the readers should emulate the patient endurance and perseverance that can be seen in Christ? Or, does it mean that Paul wants his readers to be steadfast and patient as they wait for Christ's return? One might even read it to mean the steadfastness which Christ gives to his children. More probably it means the steadfast endurance shown by our Lord as he suffered insult and injury. The practical implication would be that the Thessalonians would then, in response, also demonstrate patience and steadfastness in trials. In 1 Thessalonians 1:3 he commended his readers for their endurance; here he prays for it. That suggests that the believer never reaches perfection this side of heaven.

Personal Response

1. *What can we do so that God's word might "run" (v. 1)?*
2. *Paul says that not all people have faith. Whose fault is that (v.2)?*
3. *Can you think of ways in which God has guarded you from the evil one (v. 3)?*
4. *How ought we to respond to the "commands" given by the apostles (v.4)?*
5. *If Christ's patience is a model for us (v. 5), how would we imitate him in the rough and tumble of life?*

CHAPTER FIVE

AN ORDERLY CHRISTIAN LIFE

In the name of the Lord Jesus Christ, we command you, brothers, to keep away from every brother who is idle and does not live according to the teaching you received from us. For you yourselves know how you ought to follow our example. We were not idle when we were with you, nor did we eat anyone's food without paying for it. On the contrary, we worked night and day, laboring and toiling so that we should not be a burden to any of you. We did this, not because we do not have the right to such help, but in order to make ourselves a model for you to follow. For even when we were with you, we gave you this rule: "If a man will not work, he shall not eat." We hear that some among you are idle. They are not busy; they are busybodies. Such people we command and urge in the Lord Jesus Christ to settle down and earn the bread they eat. And as for you, brothers, never tire of doing what is right. If anyone does not obey our instruction in this letter, take special note of him. Do not associate with him, in order that he may feel ashamed. Yet do not regard him as an enemy, but warn him as a brother (2 Thess. 3:6-15).

In his first letter Paul mentions those who had stopped working, evidently thinking that the end of the age was imminent. Paul had admonished them (I Thess. 4:11f.) to go back to work and to live a quiet life, without offence to their unbelieving neighbors. It seems as if Paul's instructions had not produced the desired effect and that the situation had become even worse.

The passage before us deals with this problem. Paul counsels his readers against laziness. Also, he encourages economic independence. Without reservation he uses himself and his associates as examples for the readers to follow. Moreover, he wants the church to discipline those who live in a disorderly fashion, although he asks that they treat those who fail with kindness.

I. The Right Attitude Toward the Disorderly (vv. 6-9).

A. The Apostolic Exhortation (v. 6).

"In the name of the Lord Jesus Christ, we command you, brothers, to keep away from every brother who is idle and does not live according to the teaching you received from us."

As in verse 4 Paul uses the word "command" for his exhortations. The word "brothers," however, softens the word considerably. The fact that the commands are given in the name of the Lord Jesus Christ indicates that these instructions are not simply Paul's ideas but are given with the authority of the risen Christ.

Paul urges the Thessalonians to withdraw from every brother (or sister) who behaves in a disorderly manner. In the light of verse 15 this is not a command to excommunite such members, but to refrain from intimate fellowship with them. This denial of friendship to those who do not live according to the tradition they have received, is designed to show them the folly of their ways and bring them back to the right paths of conduct. They are still "brothers."

We have not yet been told who the "disorderly" (*ataktos*) are, but we shall see presently Paul has in mind those who have become idlers. These, he says, do not walk according to the tradition they had received. As explained in 2:15, the tradition is apostolic teaching, both oral and written, that has come down to them.

From Romans 16:17 we learn that the form of discipline suggested in our passage was to be applied not just to violators of Christian ethics but also to those who spread false teachings. "I urge you, brothers to watch out for those who cause divisions and put obstacles in your way, contrary to the teaching you have learned. Keep away from them."

B. The Apostolic Example (vv. 7-9).

1. Negatively Stated (vv. 7,8a).

"For you yourselves know how you ought to follow our example. We were not idle when we were with you, nor did we eat anyone's food without paying for it."

By reminding them that they know that idleness is not fitting for the believer he suggests that they had been given earlier teaching, but that somehow not everyone had caught its signifcance. The lifestyle of the missionaries when they founded the church in Thessalonica was a clear indication that idleness was not an approved way of life for members of the church. Although he commends them in his first letter for imitating the apostles (1:6), evidently they were not following the example of the missioners in the matter of work. Whether it was because they saw no point in working because of the notion that the coming of the Lord was so near, or whether it was the traditional aversion to work found among free Greeks, is not quite clear.

In the early church the example of the teachers and evangelists was very important, since the church had as yet very little Christian literature. For that reason Paul seems to have no inhibitions about calling on his converts to imitate him and his colleagues. In fact, he allows them no option: "you must imitate us." Preachers of the gospel may be hesitant to ask people to imitate them, but their message can be effective only if the hearers have the deep impression that the preacher sincerely strives to live up to what he is preaching.

Paul and his associates set a good example in that they

did not live in a disorderly manner when they were among them. Disorderly, in the context, seems to mean to live in idleness. The missionaries had supported themselves with the labor of their own hands (1 Thess. 2:9). They did not eat anyone's bread without paying for it. the text says simply that they did not eat bread *dorean* ("freely"). To eat bread is a Semitism for eating food (cf. Gen. 3:19), but the expression can be extended to cover maintenance in general. Whereas Paul did upon occasion accept material support, he was rather cautious in his efforts to establish new churches not to give occasion for the accusation that he was evangelizing for the sake of money.

2. Positively Stated (vv. 8b,9).

"On the contrary, we worked night and day, laboring and toiling so that we would not be a burden to any of you. We did this, not because we do not have the right to such help, but in order to make ourselves a model for you to follow."

The language here is almost identical with I Thessalonians 2:9 where Paul reminds his readers of their "toil and moil" (the word play is hard to do in English). They were careful not to sponge on other people and so worked night and day with the express purpose not to become a burden to anyone.

As in his first letter, Paul reminds the Thessalonians that the missionaries did in fact have the right to be supported by them. No doubt Paul knew what Jesus had taught in this respect, namely, that the laborer deserves his food (Matt. 10:10). However, he also knew Jesus' reminder as he sent out the twelve, "freely you have received, freely give" (Matt. 10:8). In Corinth, where he worked at the time when he wrote the Thessalonian letters, Paul also followed the policy of waiving all rights to support by his converts (1 Cor. 9:15).

Not only did the apostles not want to be a burden to their converts, but they also wanted to set a good example for them to follow. This was not simply a piece of showmanship but was a sincere attempt to go the second mile. They were to learn from the missionaries not simply to waive rights and privileges but to work hard and be economically independent of others.

II. The Admonition of the Disorderly (vv. 10-13).

A. Former Instructions Regarding Idleness (v. 10).

"For even when we were with you, we gave you this rule: 'If a man will not work, he shall not eat.'"

Not only did the apostles give the Thessalonians a good example to follow they also instructed them orally. The gist of their instruction is couched here in a pithy saying: "If a person does not wish to work, let him not even eat." Perhaps this was a proverbial saying based on Genesis 3:19, "in the sweat of your brow you shall eat bread."

We should observe carefully that Paul has people in mind who refuse to work, not those who are unemployed and would be happy to have a job by which they could earn their livelihood. But what does Paul mean when he says that those who refuse to work should not eat? Does he mean that they would be excluded from the church's support for the needy? Or, does he mean such people should not participate in the common meals of the church at which Christ's death was remembered? Perhaps it is just an observation which, as Deissmann suggests, the manager of a workshop would make: if you don't work, you won't get anything to eat.

B. Disturbing Rumors about Misconduct (v.11).

"We hear that some among you are idle. They are not busy; they are busybodies."

"We hear" is in the present tense and may suggest

something ongoing, although the present tense is sometimes used for action as a whole. The verb "to hear" would seem to indicate oral communication. However, there are examples of where something is heard via the written page as well.

Rumor had it that certain ones were walking in a disorderly manner. Paul does not charge all the members of the church with misconduct but only certain ones, whom he does not name for reasons of tact. Again the disorderly conduct seems to refer to idleness. And because they did not work they were making a public nuisance of themselves. There is a word-play in Greek that is hard to do in English: not working but working around (*ergazomai/periergazomai*), busybodies instead of being busy.

What does it mean to be a busybody? In our passage it may have a twofold meaning: trying to get their living from others and also trying to win others over to their point of view with respect-to the second advent. It could also be that because of their idleness they were keeping others from work and wasting their time. In his first letter Paul had already admonished his readers to mind their own affairs (1 Thess. 4:11). Whereas believers are encouraged to bear one another's burdens, Paul does not want them to pry into other people's lives.

C. Admonitory Directives to Idlers (v. 12).

"Such people we command and urge in the Lord Jesus Christ, to settle down and earn the bread they eat."

For the third time in this chapter (vv.1,10,12) we have the word "command." The word is softened by the next verb, "exhort" (*parakleo*), it seems, although *parakaleo* can also have a rather strong meaning. Paul's instructions are given with great authority for he speaks in the name of the "Lord Jesus Christ." On the other hand, the fact that both Paul and his readers are "in Christ" makes brothers of them all and gives this exhortation a tender tone.

In his earlier letter Paul had urged the Thessalonians to

live "quietly" (1 Thess. 4:11); here they are asked to work quietly and and eat their own bread, rather than that of others. Such a quiet kind of life is the best antidote against meddling in other people's lives.

D. Friendly Encouragement to Do What Is Right (v. 13).

"As for you, brothers, never tire of doing what is right."

The "you" stands in contrast to the idlers, and means that Paul is addressing the whole church once again. They may have grown weary in helping those who had stopped working and are now encouraged not to lose heart. We have a close parallel in Galatians 6:9, where Paul encourages the Galatians not to grow weary in welldoing, for in due time the harvest will come. Hard-working members may have felt it was not fair for them to supply the needs of the idlers, but Paul encourages them to do good to others even when they don't deserve it.

There is a word-play in our text that is hard to reproduce in English. Instead of "going bad inside" (*egkakeo*) they are to keep on "doing good" (*kalopoieo*). In any case the church as a whole is asked not to behave irresponsibly as did the idlers.

III. Discipline of the Disorderly (vv. 14, 15).

A. The Nature of the Discipline (v. 14).

"If anyone does not obey our instruction in this letter, take special note of him. Do not associate with him, in order that he may feel ashamed."

Paul isn't sure that all the members of the Thessalonian church will take his word, directed at the idlers, seriously. If his instructions are not followed, and the problem continues, then disciplinary action must be taken. First of all they must take note of such offenders. This is the only instance of the verb *semeioomai* (*nota bene*) in the New Testament, but there is a parallel in Romans 16:17, "keep an eye on those who create dissensions." It does not mean that such people shall give up their membership in the Christian community (at least not yet).

By a different punctuation some Bible translators (Luther among them) made the verse read "through a letter point him out" (to me). But the word order and the general sense of the passage is against this way of reading the text. It is highly unlikely that Paul wanted people in the church to write to him and inform on those who continued in idleness.

Not only are "the disorderly" to be marked out but they are to withdraw from fellowship with such a person. The verb *sunanamignumi* is a double compound and means they are not to get mixed up with these people. It is the same verb that is used in 1 Cor. 5:13, where the offender is to be excommunicated. Here, however, offenders are still to be treated as "brothers" (v. 15). This denial of close fellowship is designed to bring those who were offending against Christian tradition back to the paths of righteousness. People who have ignored the oral teaching of the apostles, who have treated his first letter lightly, and now also disregard the second epistle, can no longer remain in good standing in the church. They must be disciplined.

The hoped for result of this kind of denial of fellowship is that the offenders will be ashamed. The Greek verb for ashamed literally means to "turn in on oneself" (*entrepo*), and Paul, no doubt, hopes that the discipline he is suggesting will lead such people to reflect on what they are doing, repent and then again be fully accepted as members in good standing.

Discipline in the church has fallen largely into disuse, but Paul wants the entire congregation to be involved in administering discipline, although leaders must take the initiative. The apostles had learned this from Jesus (Matt. 18:15-20), the kindest person that every lived on this earth.

B. The Attitude Toward the Disciplined (v. 15).

"Yet do not regard him as an enemy, but warn him as a brother."

This verse makes it obvious that Paul is not, as in 1 Corinthians 5, talking about excommunication. The "disorderly" are not to be treated as enemies but as members of the Christian community, "brothers." However, they are to be "admonished." The verb *noutheteo* literally means "to put into mind." It can mean "rebuke" but it also has a softer side to it; perhaps "admonish" would be appropriate here.

The temptation, when discipline is carried out, is to let personal feelings of animosity enter in, and this is to be avoided. Where the church sees itself as a tightly-knit family and where membership in this family is taken seriously, discipline is an expression of love and concern for one another and can be quite effective even today.

CONCLUSION (3:16-18)

A. The Apostolic Prayer (v. 16).

"Now may the Lord of peace himself give you peace at all times and in every way. The Lord be with all of you."

This is the fourth prayer in this short epistle. It is addressed to "the Lord of peace"—an expression found only here in the New Testament. "God of peace" is more common (cf. 1 Thess. 5:23). Since Christ is divine, as far as Paul is concerned, he has no difficulty ascribing to him qualities or activities that are elsewhere ascribed to God. Perhaps Paul addresses Christ in such a way at this point because of the tension in the church about which he has just spoken. However, "peace" in the New Testament is rather broad in its compass and means more than the absence of strife. Peace means wellness and fullness of life and salvation. And Paul prays that the Lord of peace might give them peace at all times regardless of the circumstances in which they may find themselves in.

Another unique wish-prayer is: "the Lord be with all of you." To experience Christ's presence in their lives would include also his peace as a gift to them. The word "all" seems to emphasize deliberately that Paul, in spite of some sharp criticism of those who were not living up to the Christian pattern of life, holds no grudges in his heart.

B. The Authenticity of the Letter (v. 17).

"I, Paul, write this greeting in my own hand, which is the distinguishing mark in all my letters. This is how I write."

Paul regularly dictated his letters (cf. Rom. 16:22). At the end of the letter, however, he would take the pen from the hand of the amanuensis and write a greeting with his own hand. (Sometimes he adds an entire paragraph, as in Gal. 6:11ff.)

Why Paul draws attention to his signature at the end of his letters is not quite clear. From 2:2 one could infer that someone may have written a letter using Paul's name. He now alerts them to the fact that they can know that this is an authentic letter of his for he signs off in his own handwriting. It is his practice in all of his writings, he says.

C. The Christian Benediction (v. 18).

"The grace of our Lord Jesus Christ be with you all."

This benediction is identical with 1 Thessalonians 5:28, except that, once again, Paul inserts the word "all." Paul is concerned about every member of the church, even those who have stumbled and failed. The letter began with the wish-prayer that God's grace might be sufficient for the needs of the church, and it ends on the same note. Grace, the undeserved favor and kindness of God, manifested in Christ, is one of Paul's fundamental themes. He never seems to grow tired of proclaiming the good news of God's grace.

Personal Response

1. *Is self-supporting ministry still an option today (v. 8)?*
2. *What should guide a church in its support of its ministers?*
3. *How should we treat those who seemingly cannot make it economically?*
4. *Is the pattern of discipline outlined in our text possible in our congregations today?*
5. *What are the steps in discipline outlined by Jesus in Matthew 18:15-20?*

SELECTED ENGLISH LANGUAGE COMMENTARIES ON THE THESSALONIANS

Best, E. *A Commentary on the First and Second Epistles of the Thessalonians*. New York: Harper, 1972.

Bruce, F.F. *I and II Thessalonians*. Waco: Word, 1982.

Ewert, David. "I and II Thessalonians," in *Evangelical Commentary on the Bible*, ed. Walter A. Elwell. Grand Rapids: Baker Book House, 1989.

Frame, J.E. *A Critical and Exegestical Commentary on the Epistles of St. Paul to the Thessalonians*. ICC. New York: Charles Scribner's Sons, 1912.

Grayston, K. *The Letters of Paul to the Philippians and to the Thessalonians*. Cambridge: Cambridge University Press, 1967.

Harris, W.B. *I and II Thessalonians*. London: Epworth, 1968.

Hendriksen, W. *Exposition of I and II Thessalonians*. Grand Rapids: Baker, 1955.

Hiebert, D.E. *The Thessalonian Epistles*. Chicago: Moody Press, 1971.

Marshall, I.H. *I and II Thessalonians*. Grand Rapids: Eerdmans, 1983.

Milligan, G. *St. Paul's Epistles to the Thessalonians*. Reprint. Grand Rapids: Eerdmans, 1952.

Moore, A.L. *I and II Thessalonians*. Greenwood: Attic Press, 1969

Morris, L. *The First and Second Epistles to the Thessalonians*. Grand Rapids: Eerdmans, 1959.

Stott, John R.W. *The Gospel and the End of Time: The Message of I and II Thessalonians*. Downers Grove: InterVarsity, 1991.

Thomas, R.L. "I and II Thessalonians" in *The Expositor's Bible Commentary*. Grand Rapids: Zondervan, 1978.

Wanamaker, C.A. *The Epistles to the Thessalonians: A Commentary on the Greek Text*. Grand Rapids: Eerdmans, 1990.

Ward, R.A. *Commentary on 1 and 2 Thessalonians*. Waco: Word, 1973.